W9-CRK-754

THE WORKS OF TA'UNGA

No. 2 of the Pacific History Series
General Editor: H. E. Maude
Literary Adviser: J. W. Davidson

THE WORKS OF TA'UNGA

RECORDS OF A POLYNESIAN TRAVELLER
IN THE SOUTH SEAS, 1833-1896

❧❧❧

R. G. and Marjorie Crocombe

With annotations by
Jean Guiart, Niel Gunson, and Dorothy Shineberg

Canberra
AUSTRALIAN NATIONAL UNIVERSITY PRESS

UNIVERSITY OF HAWAII PRESS
Honolulu

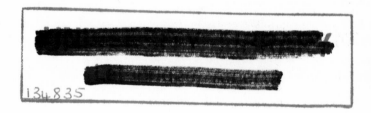

134835

The Pacific History Series of books provides an outlet for the publication of original manuscripts important to historians and others interested in the Pacific islands, as well as bibliographies and other aids to Pacific studies.

No. 1 in the series was:

A Cruize in a Queensland Labour Vessel to the South Seas, by W. E. Giles, edited by Deryck Scarr (1968).

Other volumes in course of preparation include:

The Marquesan Journal of Edward Robarts, 1797-1806, edited by Gregory Dening.

The Fijian Diary and Narrative of Edwin J. Turpin, edited by A. I. Diamond.

Account of Trading Voyages in the Western Pacific, 1841-1844, by Andrew Cheyne, edited by Dorothy Shineberg.

For

the new generation of

leaders of change

in the

South Pacific

FOREWORD

The publication of *The Works of Ta'unga* is perhaps a fitting reminder that almost exactly half a century has now passed since the modern study of Pacific history commenced with the publication of Scholefield's pioneering classic *The Pacific: Its Past and Future, and the Policy of the Great Powers from the Eighteenth Century.* The very title of that work epitomises the historical certainties of its era: the important theme in historiography was then to chronicle and interpret the struggle of the European nations to carve out the Pacific for their mutual benefit. But, as Professor John M. Ward so ingenuously remarks of a later work: 'It was weak on the islands themselves'.

In the ensuing years we have moved so far from this position that some of us might feel more at home with our colleagues in sister disciplines such as anthropology, geography, and archaeology than with the products of some of the more conservative schools of history. In general we have lost our innate belief in the natural right of Europeans to dominate politically, culturally, or economically, and with its disappearance has come a realisation that much of our historical writing has in fact been ethnocentric to the verge of apologetics. In consequence the subject of our study is increasingly becoming the people of the Pacific themselves, their pre-European past as revealed by archaeology, linguistics, and ethnohistory, and many of the natural sciences such as ecology, and their post-contact response to the increasing pressure of outside cultural influences.

Like all historians, however, we are still dependent on documentary sources to a greater extent than other social scientists, and to our dismay we have come to realise that in the Pacific our sources are to a large extent tainted, being written by

Europeans possessing the almost inescapable bias of their racial background. Only in the occasional transculturite — a Mariner, Robarts or O'Connell — do we find a degree of integration, or even identification, sufficient to overcome this legacy and achieve objectivity, though not necessarily understanding, in their writings.

Hence there has been a deliberate attempt during the past few years to discover vernacular works and make them available for the use of scholars. It is not easy: the number of texts is limited — confined to Polynesia and Micronesia, while the ravages of tropical climate and insects coupled with neglect by acculturated descendants has resulted in the destruction of all but a few. Even where discovered, however, they are necessarily mute to the vast majority of us until translated, and, where necessary, explained, by the rare scholar skilled in the local language and steeped in the local cultural and traditional background.

The indigenous writers of Hawaii, New Zealand, and Tahiti have been the first to be translated and published, as witness the recent fine editions of the historical essays of John Papa I'i and Samuel M. Kamakau, but the production of an annotated collection of the works of Ta'unga represents a new breakthrough as being the first book by a nineteenth-century author from central or western Polynesia to be published, and the first by any Pacific islander, with I think the sole exception of the manuscript 'Life of Auna', to be written about any country other than his own.

The book could never have been produced without the local knowledge and, above all, the sheer pertinacity of Ron and Marjorie Crocombe. Both ethnohistorians familiar with the language and culture of the Cook Islands, and one a Rarotongan born only a few miles from Ta'unga's birthplace, they laboriously collected, over a number of years, every scrap of material which they were able to discover either written by Ta'unga or about him. And then in the few hours that could be spared from their busy lives — the one as Executive Officer in charge of the New Guinea Research Unit and the other teaching Pacific history as well as writing and broadcasting — they translated this material and pieced it, together with other information, into a coherent whole which not only reproduces Ta'unga's surviving writings in their entirety (apart from duplications) but also serves as a biography of the remarkable man himself.

Although our main thanks are therefore due to this gifted pair, they would be the first to acknowledge that their work would have been less effective had they not been fortunate in securing the generous collaboration of no less than three leading subject specialists, each of whom read the manuscript critically and prepared annotations where such seemed to be required. Professor Jean Guiart, the authority on the anthropology of New Caledonia, has identified wherever possible the people and places referred to by Ta'unga in his often obscure Rarotongan transliterations of New Caledonian words, as well as commenting on the value and correctness of many of his ethnographical observations; Niel Gunson, the authority on Protestant missions and missionaries, has illuminated many obscure passages in the text from his unrivalled knowledge of mission documentation; while Dorothy Shineberg, the authority on Melanesian trading relations, whose definitive book on the sandalwood trade will have appeared before this work is published, has in her notes placed Ta'unga's stay in New Caledonia and the Loyalty Islands in the perspective of the general contact history of the period. Last, but not least, Jennifer Terrell has exercised her editorial skill by pulling the work of so much individual talent together.

The Works of Ta'unga is an important book because it gives us a picture of the central and western Pacific at a time of immense cultural change due to the impact on the hitherto relatively stabilised local societies of two powerful forces: one moving from the east and the other from the west. And uniquely, for it may be doubted if there is another such manuscript in existence, it gives the picture from the recipient's side.

Moving west from Tahiti was the increasingly confident army of militant Christianity, of which Ta'unga was one of the small advance party of reconnaissance scouts, expendable if necessary; they were the sowers of the seed that was ultimately to be harvested by the main body led by the more professionally trained European missionaries. From the bustling wharves of Sydney, on the other hand, there were simultaneously moving east the vanguards of commerce, equally confident of success as they developed the trading potentialities of the various island groups, exchanging the products of England's industrial revolution for salt pork, sandalwood, bêche-de-mer and any other island product from which profit might be made. As Ta'unga's narrative shows in

somewhat gruesome detail, the advance parties of this army
were also apt to be expendable.

The beachcombers — that motley and often rapscallion
collection of escapees or deviants from western society, prepared to conform to island norms in return for permission
to live with their island hosts — had by and large seen their
heyday by Ta'unga's time, and only in Rotuma does he
mention their continued presence and influence: their
opposition to the missionaries and the fact that the Rotumans
now had 'an extensive knowledge of the English language'.
Niue was still opposing the landing of any stranger, missionary
or otherwise, largely through a justifiable fear of introduced
disease, a fear that was to keep a few islands such as Rennell
and Bellona inviolate right into the present century.

Elsewhere, however, in the period between the beachcomber
and the coming of European political domination, the two
acculturative forces of missionary and trader were fighting for
ascendancy over the Pacific islander; and nowhere do we see
the interplay more clearly than in the pages of Ta'unga. In the
east, from Tahiti to Samoa, the battle had largely been won
by the Christian forces, or at least (as in Samoa) a truce
declared, but in Melanesia the pioneer missionaries and the
sandalwooders were still at loggerheads. We get here an
intimate picture of the mutual recriminations: for example,
the charges and counter-charges over such matters as the
introduction of disease, for which both parties were presumably responsible and neither to blame.

To the anthropologist Ta'unga gives a portrayal of New
Caledonian and Loyalty Islands society before it had been
affected other than superficially by contact with the outside
world: as he insists himself, he writes as one who has seen
what he describes with his own eyes and not through second-
hand descriptions by native informants. Biased as Ta'unga
often is by his own beliefs, he has nevertheless given us the
first detailed description of Melanesian society that we possess,
and, even if imperfect by the standards of modern professional
ethnography, it cannot be ignored by future students.

Above all, however, Ta'unga's works are worth reading for
their own sake, as revealing the thoughts and deeds of a
Polynesian, descended from a noble line of priests, who fully
justified in his life the labours of his missionary teachers;
utterly single-minded and sincere, he was at once courageous
and humane, obstinate and lovable — just so must have been
many of the early missionaries to the tribes of Europe.

Fortunately for us Ta'unga was writing in the earliest, and I submit the finest, age of Polynesian literature, when the recounting of oral epics was still an art which facilitated the graphic expression of ideas; and many new writers, as yet undismayed by what was later to appear (happily only for a time) as an overwhelming inferiority to the European, were anxious to try out their skill in composition. As a result he writes naturally and entirely without self-consciousness, with all the freshness of early English prose. To conclude, *The Works of Ta'unga* is not only an important primary source for the student of Pacific history or anthropology; it possesses the additional merit of being an absorbing literary treat.

H. E. Maude

PREFACE

A great deal of the wave of culture change which swept across the Pacific in the nineteenth century was generated by Christian missions. It is not generally realised, however, that the introduction of the Christian religion to most Pacific islands was the work, not of European missionaries, but of many hundreds of Tahitian, Rarotongan, Samoan, and other Polynesian mission teachers. After attending relatively short courses of instruction under English mentors who were based successively in the Society Islands, Rarotonga, and Samoa, the indigenous evangelists of the London Missionary Society particularly were dispersed to the myriads of islands scattered far and wide across the Pacific Ocean to spread the teachings with which they themselves had so recently become acquainted.

To understand the nature of the contact situation, then, one needs to know something of the indigenous teachers who acted as mediators between the traditional societies and the new culture. We need to know their background, their knowledge and beliefs, their aspirations and their methods of work. It was they who witnessed the early stages of culture change at first hand, and who lived with the people of the islands to which they were sent, where they often learned their languages and the nuances of their cultures. Ta'unga was one of these early Polynesian missionaries; a perceptive observer and a prolific writer who took the trouble to record, as he himself phrased it, 'What I saw with my eyes, heard with my ears, and felt with my hands'.[1]

Our introduction to Ta'unga was accidental, and the five-year task of dovetailing his story together has remained a labour of love fitted into evenings and weekends as well as

[1]Ta'unga 1879.

during field trips for other purposes. In 1960 we asked the Polynesian Society for photocopies of certain vernacular manuscripts, and Ta'unga's 1879 manuscript (which was not catalogued in the Polynesian Society Library and which we did not know existed) was accidentally copied along with them. This vivid description of life on New Caledonia before any white man had ever lived there constituted the earliest written source on that island by anyone with a command of a local language, or with experience of actual residence there. It whetted our appetites to know more, not only about New Caledonia in that early phase of culture contact, but also about the man who so eloquently recorded this colourful episode. The Polynesian Society Library was then only partly catalogued and they were unable to locate any further material by Ta'unga, but they invited us to search for ourselves. This we did the following year and found four more manuscripts (1846a, 1847a, 1862, and 1870). For nearly two years we studied the extensive microfilm records of the London Missionary Society and found considerable material by him and about him, including his manuscripts of 1833, 1842c, and 1847b. Several visits to the Mitchell Library revealed more information about him from Pitman's diaries and other sources, as well as Ta'unga's writings dated 1842. Letters to a number of libraries and institutions revealed the 1846b paper in the New York Public Library as well as references to Ta'unga from a number of sources.

Systematic perusal of relevant books and periodicals, and correspondence with a wide range of people (who were invariably helpful) led to the location of further material by and about him. A visit to the Cook Islands late in 1961 enabled us to gather oral traditions about Ta'unga in the islands today and to collect material relating to him from the Land Court, the Cook Islands Christian Church, and a number of individuals. An examination of records in the Bishop Museum and the University of Hawaii Library in 1964 produced still more new data, and during a visit to Samoa in 1965 Pastor Fiti Sunia told us about the tradition of Ta'unga's visit to heaven. The flow of correspondence which has revealed so much over the past years has now ceased to bring new material to light and we feel that the time to publish has come.

We are often asked why Ta'unga wrote. Why does anybody? Ascribing motives is easy, but testing their validity almost impossible. We nevertheless offer the following comments.

The art of writing was introduced to Ta'unga's island of Rarotonga when he was a young lad. It was a highly prized skill and he excelled at it. It was his handwriting that was sent to London in 1833 to demonstrate the success of this aspect of the mission's work.[2] Charles Pitman,[3] who was Ta'unga's mentor, kept an extensive daily diary, as well as writing regular reports to his London headquarters and preparing a journal on his every voyage. Almost every English missionary of the day did likewise. Ta'unga came into contact with many of them and it is likely that they encouraged his talent in this direction. Though he could not have read what they wrote (for he never learnt English) he was certainly aware that they did write. Several of his earlier writings are addressed to Pitman personally though Ta'unga would have known that Pitman read many of his letters aloud to the whole congregation of Ta'unga's home district.

Some of his writings were strictly functional. His vocabulary of the Tuauru language (1842d) was compiled to enable new teachers to know something of the language before their arrival, and his booklets (1847c, d) were written for use as textbooks in the school he intended to establish on his return to New Caledonia.

The flow of letters to Thomas Powell from 1849 to 1872 kept his immediate superior informed of affairs at the Manu'a Station which constituted part of Powell's district.[4] A considerable part of his 1862 manuscript was directed at the youths of his home island, exhorting them to adhere to Christian teachings and pleading with them to offer themselves as missionaries. The manuscripts of 1870 and 1871 were replies to requests for information from English missionaries, and his 1879 manuscript was addressed to W. Wyatt Gill, the missionary ethnographer-historian with whom Ta'unga was then collaborating in the translation of the Bible. Gill was

[2]Ta'unga 1833a.
[3]The Reverend Charles Pitman (1796-1884) had received more schooling than most of his colleagues and had begun to study Latin before being trained as a missionary at Gosport Academy. At Ngatangiia from 1827 to 1855 he worked at translating the Bible. A scholarly and patient man, though sickly, he proved an able mentor to Ta'unga. — N.G.
[4]The Reverend Thomas Powell spent most of his life stationed on Tutuila. As in the case of his colleague, the Reverend George Pratt, his study of the Samoan language led him to take a great interest in Samoan narratives and cultural lore. His valuable manuscripts were published in part by Dr John Fraser in the journals of the Polynesian Society and the Royal Society of New South Wales. — N.G.

an avid collector and writer and it is probable that he requested Ta'unga to record his reminiscences of his early life in New Caledonia.[5]

Ta'unga's main contributions to the history of the Pacific are his accounts of village life and culture contact in New Caledonia and the Loyalty Islands (which are among the earliest in existence), and his clear statements of his own beliefs and attitudes which give a rare insight into the perception and motivation of Polynesian missionaries of the period.

In translation we have tried as far as possible to preserve Ta'unga's own style, though slight changes of grammar and punctuation have been made. It must be remembered that his own formal education was limited to several years under an untrained teacher. The only orthography he knew was that used by his European teachers for reducing the Rarotongan language to writing. Only about fifteen letters were used and many of the forms and sounds used in the Tuauru language of the south-west corner of New Caledonia were quite foreign to Rarotongan. When Ta'unga wrote Tuauru words therefore (and he was probably the first person ever to do so) he had to use the letters which had the nearest equivalent value in Rarotongan. Rarotongan does not use the letters b, d, g, h, j, w, and y which are common in Tuauru and related dialects. Thus Ta'unga wrote Purupare for Burupwari (the French often use a corruption of their own by spelling it Boulouparis), Gomaniu for Komwainyu, Jeiue for Yeiw (in this case Ta'unga introduced the letter j, probably after consulting English missionaries). Moreover, all Rarotongan words end in a vowel, and when a Tuauru word did not end in a vowel Ta'unga invariably added one: for example Wanakam which he wrote as Uanakakame.

Personal names are in the language of the person named, with Ta'unga's spelling of them in brackets after the first use. Where the identification is not certain, Ta'unga's spelling is used with the suggested identification in a footnote. Place names are given in the form used in the British Admiralty Naval Intelligence Division's *Geographical Handbook on the*

[5]The Reverend William Wyatt Gill (1828-96) was one of the first university graduates to serve as a London Missionary Society missionary in the Pacific. After serving on Mangaia from 1852 to 1872 he spent a second term at Rarotonga between 1877 and 1883. Deeply interested in the ethnology and folklore of the Polynesians he wrote a number of books and contributed articles to learned journals. — N.G.

Pacific Islands, and those not included in the handbook are given in the form accepted in the locality concerned.

The source text is indicated at the beginning of each chapter or episode but in several instances we have presented composite accounts, using the most comprehensive manuscript as the basic document and interpolating additional material from other manuscripts in appropriate places. To have given full translations of all his writings on each topic would have been tedious as there is considerable overlap, and to have presented the manuscripts one after the other would have made comprehension of topics and episodes difficult because each deals with a variety of matters in no particular pattern or sequence. Where composite accounts are given the date or dates and page numbers of the relevant manuscript or manuscripts are shown in brackets at the end of the passage. In the few instances where facts or opinions differ between manuscripts this is explained in footnotes.

Where known the present location of manuscripts is shown in the list of references. A microfilm copy of all the manuscripts we have located, and of the translations of them, has been prepared by the Department of Pacific History, Australian National University, Canberra. Inquiries about purchasing copies should be directed to that department.

R.G.C. and M.C.

ACKNOWLEDGMENTS

Foremost among the many people whose assistance has enabled the completion of this book is of course Ta'unga himself, for, had he not taken such pains to record his impressions and opinions, there would be nothing to write. He was a man of courage and intelligence and was possessed of a charismatic personality which seemed to infect everyone with whom he had contact. Each new manuscript, each new fact which has come to light, has served to enhance our respect for him, as an observer, as a religious leader, and as a man.

To his descendants, too, we are deeply indebted. To Ngapoko Terei, Ta'unga's eldest surviving grand-daughter who now holds the title of Terei Mataiapo, to the Iro family, to Mrs Paiau Short, Mrs G. Crummer and many other relatives we are obliged for the generous way in which they gave their time and knowledge to assist in the completion of this project.

We are most grateful to Messrs Taira Rere and Joseph Vati for carefully checking translations and suggesting improvements. Others in the islands who kindly gave assistance include Mr C. T. Cowan (Tau Puru Ariki), Judge H. J. Morgan, the Reverend B. T. Thorogood, Pastor Toka, the Reverend Hugh Neems, Pastor Fiti Sunia, Dr John A. Numa, and Mr Ta'i Tekeu.

Without the example and constant encouragement of Mr Harry Maude we would never have tackled this task, and without the support and interest of Professor J. W. Davidson and the generous resources of the Australian National University it could not have been undertaken.

The biographical sketches of missionaries which are contained in many of the notes in the early chapters particularly were kindly provided by Dr Niel Gunson, and both he and

Dr Dorothy Shineberg provided a great deal of valuable advice and information. Notes specifically contributed by either of them are acknowledged by the initials N.G. or D.S. at the end of the note. Mrs Jennifer Terrell checked the manuscript in meticulous detail, collated and developed a number of footnotes, and suggested various improvements in textual editing. The maps were drawn by Mr Hans Gunther.

We are deeply obliged to Dr J. Cumpston and Professor Jean Guiart for detailed criticism of material relating to New Caledonia and the Loyalty Islands, and to Mr Petro Atiti, Dr Lowell Holmes, Mr R. P. Gilson, Dr D. McTaggart, Dr Peter Pirie, Mr Alistair Hall, Samuela Mana Ariki, and Mr Fred Dunn for historical and geographical data. Professor Guiart and Mr Atiti also advised on the spelling and identification of New Caledonian proper names. For access to manuscripts by and relating to Ta'unga we are grateful to the London Missionary Society, the Polynesian Society, the Alexander Turnbull Library, the Mitchell Library, the National Library of Australia, the New York Public Library, the Bishop Museum, and the University of Hawaii.

To all the above persons and institutions, and to any whose names may have been inadvertently omitted, we wish to express our sincere thanks.

R.G.C. and M.C.

Port Moresby
September 1967

CONTENTS

page

Foreword, by H. E. Maude ix

Preface xv

Acknowledgments xxi

Abbreviations xxv

1 The Historical Setting 1

2 The Westward Voyage 10

3 Establishing the Tuauru Mission 27

4 The *Star* Massacre 43

5 The Yate Incident 55

6 The Epidemics 59

7 An Attack from the Isle of Pines 63

8 Spreading the Word 69

9 The Loyalty Islands 77

10 On the Eating of Men 86

11 On the Work of the Gods 96

12 Customs Miscellaneous 102

13 Return to Rarotonga 112

14 Samoa 117

15 Success and Tribulation in the Manu'a Church 126

16 Samoan Miscellany 138

17 The Declining Years 143

References 149

Index 157

FIGURES

		page
1	Map of Rarotonga, Cook Islands	4
2	The Titikaveka chapel, which Ta'unga helped to build	8
3	The *Camden*, which carried the missionaries on the western voyage	11
4	Map of the South Pacific islands showing the route of Ta'unga's voyage on the *Camden*	13
5	Niue canoe	14
6	Map of New Caledonia and the Loyalty Islands	28
7	A chief's house	33
8	The palisaded dwelling of Matuku at Gadji	46
9	Isle of Pines canoe	65
10	Beginning and ending of Ta'unga's letter to Pitman from Nengone	88-9
11	Missionary representation of the son of Pasan asking his father for the fat man to eat	94
12	Bags containing relics of ancestors	97
13	New Caledonian weapons	113
14	A Tuauru man, probably Navie	115
15	Map of Samoa	118
16	The old church at Manu'a	120

ABBREVIATIONS

The following abbreviations are used in the footnotes and references:

CTC	C. T. Cowan, Rarotonga
LMS	London Missionary Society, London
ML	Mitchell Library, Sydney
NLC	Native Land Court, Rarotonga
NT	Ngapoko Terei, Rarotonga
PRO	Public Record Office, London
PS	Polynesian Society, Wellington
RPG	R.P. Gilson Papers, Australian National University, Canberra
SSJ	South Seas Journals, LMS
SSL	South Seas Letters, LMS
SSR	South Seas Reports, LMS

1

THE HISTORICAL SETTING

In every tribe of old Polynesia there was a class of men who specialised in religious and ritual matters. They were well versed in the practical arts of agriculture, construction, and seamanship, but more important still was their knowledge of the esoteric — the ability to invoke the aid of the gods, to bring spiritual support to temporal activities, and to interpret the very meaning and purpose of life itself. They were men of skill and of vision, and are often referred to in English as priests, but as the term has a somewhat restricted connotation we shall adhere to their indigenous title — *ta'unga*.[1]

Eight or nine hundred years ago by genealogical reckoning, a tribe headed by the chief Pou-te-vananga-roa lived on the island of Raiatea.[2] One of the *ta'unga* of that tribe was a man named Makanakura and his title name was More-ta'unga-o-te-tini. According to Rarotongan tradition, the population of Raiatea had grown rapidly since the island was first peopled by sea-borne immigrants from the original homeland of Hawaiki, and its valleys had filled with people. Hunger had at times necessitated the rigid assertion of rights of ownership, and the tenets of hospitality were then set aside in a more basic struggle for survival. At such a time of shortage, we are told, a dispute arose between Tutapu and Tangiia, the two

[1]*Ta'unga* is the Rarotongan form. The dialectal equivalents in Hawaii and New Zealand were *kahuna* and *tohunga* respectively. There were, of course, differences of role and function between the priests of the various Polynesian subcultures, but in all cases the priests were quite distinct from the spirit mediums, who were known in Rarotonga as *taura atua*.

[2]This history of the period preceding European contact was derived from the following sources: Native Land Court 1903-13, vol. 4, pp. 124-8 and vol. 7, pp. 192-4; Savage 1916, p. 7; Terei and Savage n.d., pp. 3-5, and 1916 *passim;* Tamarua 1892, p. 93; Taraare *c.*1870, *passim;* Terei 1899, pp. 1-3, 1905, pp. 1-4, and 1909, p. 9.

adopted sons of the chief Pou-te-vananga-roa. Their quarrel was centred on disagreement over their respective rights to the fruit of a particular breadfruit tree, though their rival claims to their father's title and lands were obviously the more fundamental cause of the trouble. The conflict developed into a series of skirmishes, and as time went by more and more people became involved on the one side or the other. Eventually, when it was apparent that the odds were against him, Tangiia and his followers left their former homeland and put to sea to find themselves a new island. Tangiia's party was very large, though just how numerous we cannot say, and in it there were six *ta'unga,* one of whom was More-ta'unga-o-te-tini.

After a long and eventful journey the party reached the island of Rarotonga where they were received hospitably by the descendants of those other Polynesians who had settled there several centuries earlier. Tangiia and his followers gained political ascendancy over these people and took some of their women as wives. They then divided the lands of the island so that every family received a share, and a portion of land on the eastern side of the island in the sub-district of Ngati Au, adjacent to the land of the high chief Pa-te-ariki-upoko-tini, was allotted to More-ta'unga-o-te-tini.

On the death of Makanakura, the title of More-ta'unga-o-te-tini passed to More-mavete-ki-te-Rangi and thence over the succeeding centuries in the following patrilineal order:

More aruru rangi
More maranga rangi
More ta'unga
More mouitekura
More te aratoa o Avaiki
More maa
More apai atua
More papa ati
More mimiti nui
More vaevae onu (kura a te rau)
More pa atua
More rapa atua
More noo marae
More ta'unga
More kura a te rau
More vaereanga rangi
More tinokura teangungu
More uri tatea

More kiti (kaitangata)
More okotai
More kaputeue.[3]

While much of note happened during those centuries, it was all within the framework of the known institutions, the accepted techniques, and the unquestioned beliefs of the islanders. But in the year 1797 a strange vessel appeared off the island's reef, larger, taller, and better equipped by far than the canoes to which they were accustomed. She did not stay long, but some of the island people went aboard her to witness for themselves the marvels of this 'floating island'. There was a carving on her stern in the pattern BOUNTY, but its significance was lost to them.[4] In later years several other ships sailed by, and speculation as to the nature and origins of these vessels and the white-skinned beings who sailed them may well have necessitated some modifications to beliefs about the nature of the world and the forces at work within it.

In 1814 the island people had the opportunity to study white men closer at hand, and to find, among other things, that these were no gods, though they were indeed a strange race of mortals; for in that year the schooner *Cumberland* anchored at the island for three months while she loaded a cargo of yellow dye-wood.[5] Among the extensive list of things learned from the crew of the *Cumberland* was the existence of two great new gods — Tiova (Jehovah) and Tititarai (Jesus Christ) — whose power was great in heaven or earth.[6]

At the time of the visit of the *Cumberland* the More title was held by Kaputeue, but as he was without living male issue it was necessary to find an heir who could inherit the title when the time came. Kaputeue's grandfather, More Kiti, had had a second wife who was the daughter of the chief Tangiiau, and from her had been born the warrior Vaereangarangi. He in turn begat Teariki Taia, who was a growing young man at the time of the *Cumberland's* stay. Teariki Taia subsequently married and his first child, a son, was born in or about the year 1818. As this child was the first-born descendant of the next most senior branch of the family, it was decided that, after the passing of Kaputeue, the title

[3]Terei 1905. It should be noted that this genealogy differs in some minor details from his manuscript of 1899.
[4]For a description of the *Bounty*'s visit see Maude 1958, pp. 121-4.
[5]See Maude and Crocombe 1962.
[6]Maretu 1871.

should fall on him, and they named him accordingly More-
ta'unga-o-te-tini. This was a rather cumbersome name for
daily use and he was generally known for the rest of his life
simply as Ta'unga.

In August 1796 the mission ship *Duff* sailed from London,
and travelled more than half way round the globe until she
reached Tahiti. There her passengers, members of the
Missionary Society (afterwards known as the London Missionary Society or LMS), established the first permanent centre of
Christian teaching in Polynesia. After nearly two decades of
slow progress with its evangelistic work, the mission was
suddenly given a new impetus when Christianity was adopted
as a national religion by the Tahitian ruler. Churches were
soon formed and the energies of the younger converts were
channelled into opening new mission areas. The church at
Raiatea, under the direction of the missionaries L. E. Threlkeld and John Williams, played an enthusiastic role in this
expansion and after initial success at Rurutu set aside two
teachers, Papeiha and Vahapata, for Aitutaki in 1821. When
Williams and his colleague Robert Bourne from Tahaa 'discovered' Rarotonga in 1823,[7] Papeiha of Raiatea was left there
and joined several months later by Rio. They established
their headquarters in Avarua on the north coast of the island,

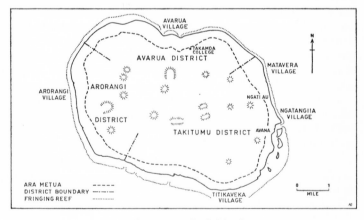

1   Rarotonga, Cook Islands

[7]Williams and his colleagues took the credit for 'discovering' Rarotonga
despite the fact that the island had been visited previously by the *Bounty*
mutineers and Captain Goodenough. See Maude and Crocombe 1962.

and set up a mission village there.[8] Many inquirers flocked to this village and built themselves new homes there, but it is doubtful whether the little boy Ta'unga or his parents ventured near the centre of the new religion, for most of the *ta'unga* were violently opposed to the new beliefs.[9] But by 1827 much of the opposition had been overcome and a new mission settlement was set up at Ngatangiia, right in the district where Ta'unga lived.

In the following year the mission ship returned, this time bringing English missionaries to reside on the island. Charles Pitman, the missionary who took charge of the Ngatangiia district, organised the laying out of a new village, and house-sites were allotted on either side of a newly-formed road along the coast. The various families left their own lands and moved to the coast to build anew in this village. Pitman's next task was to establish a school, and to it both the children and the adults of the village flocked, seeking the wondrous rewards which, they hoped, would be available to those who mastered the secrets of the white man's words.[10] And among the brightest and most diligent of them Pitman soon came to notice a young lad named Ta'unga.

Once the Ngatangiia school was firmly established, Pitman wished to extend mission influence to the district of Titika-veka, for the people there had resisted the new religion longer than any others on the island. So in 1832, after only four years' schooling and at the age of about fourteen years, Ta'unga was appointed to take classes for the children of Titikaveka. At the same time an older man, Iro by name, was appointed to teach the adults there, and every morning at sunrise Ta'unga and Iro walked from Ngatangiia to Titika-veka to take their classes.[11]

Their work met with rapid success, and one of the Titika-veka chiefs gave a portion of land on which a chapel was built. Later on, at the people's insistence, Ta'unga and Iro built houses for themselves in Titikaveka and resided there

[8]This chapter of events is fully described by Papeiha *c.*1830 and Williams and Bourne 1823.

[9]This was not always the case. In Tahiti there were several priests among the earlier converts and Ellis (1831, vol. 1, p. 233) remarked that converts from the Arioi society made the best teachers. One of the most notable was the former priest Aura. — N.G.

[10]Prout 1843, p. 248; Williams 1837, p. 103.

[11]Pitman to London Missionary Society (LMS) 26.8.1841, South Seas Letters of the London Missionary Society (abbreviated hereafter to SSL).

with their new flock. Ta'unga remained Pitman's star pupil,
and in July 1833 Pitman proudly despatched to his London
headquarters a 'specimen of the writing of a Native lad about
fourteen years of age named Ta'unga'.[12]

In September 1833 Ta'unga wrote the following statement
of his views on Christianity and sent them to Pitman.

God showed great love in giving his beloved son to the
world. If he had refused to give his son, men could not have
lived on. The real reason for our life lies in the death of Jesus.
The shedding of his blood made God angry. Had it not been
for that blood men could not have found goodness. Satan's
desires would have triumphed and all men would have ended
in eternal darkness. It was the boundless anger of God and
the sins of man which descended upon Jesus. The anger of
God did not strike mankind because Jesus became a shield
against the anger of his Father, and Jesus carried the burden
and so he was overcome by death. Thus mankind was saved
because he took death upon himself. He died because he
wanted mankind to live on. Thus goodness was achieved and
mankind was given life, and so it is said that man lives
because of the death of Jesus. His death was sanctified and
man lived.

While living in heaven at the side of his Father he decided
to come to this world. What he really wanted was that mankind should live. He was going to die so that mankind might
achieve the good life. When he died, he and his Father
made a promise of love in the heavens. When he had decided
that he should die, nothing at all was omitted, everything
was provided for, from his childhood onwards. He never
flinched, he had made up his mind he was going to die, and
he did die. His goal was achieved.

Now it is my desire that every man should respect his
blood, that it may become remembered throughout the world.
In order for this remembrance to come about, the word of
God must be spread throughout every single island so that
every person may reach heaven and sit at the side of Jesus
so that there might be boundless joy.

The two crucial things are the anger of God and boundless
love. Because of his anger with man for his committing sin,

[12]Pitman to LMS 15.7.1833, SSL. The writing was a transcription, in
Rarotongan, of a portion of the Gospel according to St Mark, and is
referred to in the References as Ta'unga 1833a.

souls went down to Hell, but because of his great love, God brought men back from the fire, and the souls reached heaven, and joined with the sacred ones who became friends with them.

Because of his great love God gave his son and made him into a man so as to carry away the sins of man. Thus the good people achieved all things. His blood washed away our sins. As the number of people who yearn to sanctify his blood increases so God's happiness with those people will increase, and eventually perhaps all men will arrive above in heaven. It is my great wish that all men should do so, that they should be ashamed of their evil ways and return to the good, to abandon wrong and to follow the way of the children of the light so that God might be overjoyed, and all the angels too. The good people will see the great glory of God and shall live with him for ever after.[13]   ⤳

Within three years of writing the above, Ta'unga was at odds with the mission as a result of the marked divergence between Rarotongan and mission ideas of sexual morality. While the local code expected a young man to express his virility, the mission prescribed strict abstinence for the un-married. A Titakaveka woman, Teanini by name, bore a son to Ta'unga and he was named Daniela or Daniel. Iro adopted the child and cared for him.[14]

Ta'unga was dismissed by Pitman, but soon repented and sought readmission to the church and reappointment to his teaching post. He wrote Pitman several letters expressing his regrets, and also visited him to explain his 'distress of mind'. Pitman exhorted him to more consistent conduct in future, and, before departing for a visit to Tahiti, urged the church elders to converse frequently with Ta'unga and to 'be faithful in pointing out the heinousness of his sin'.[15] He was, as Pitman noted, 'a lad of very promising talents', and before long he was restored to his former position.

[13]Ta'unga 1833b. This statement of faith shows Ta'unga had a sound grasp of the doctrine taught by the missionaries and that it supplied him with a missionary dynamic. It compares most favourably with other testimonies. Ta'unga was to develop his missionary philosophy in the field and saw the sin of vengeance as the root cause of all that he deplored in Melanesian society (see p. 108). All Ta'unga's teachings were in keeping with his original confession (see p. 37). — N.G.

[14]Native Land Court, vol. 1, p. 228; Tamarua 1892, p. 93. Daniel died as a young lad during an epidemic of dysentery.

[15]Pitman to LMS 21.7.1835, SSL.

When the London Missionary Society opened a theological college at Takamoa on the north coast of the island in 1839, they proposed to train indigenous missionaries not only for service in Rarotonga and the neighbouring islands, but also to carry the gospel westward to the still heathen islands of Melanesia. Ta'unga was among those young men who were anxious to enter the college, but he was then a little too young to commence training. During 1840 he continued his teaching work and his private studies, and on his own initiative undertook the translation of the account of the journeys of the Children of Israel from Tahitian into Rarotongan.[16] Ta'unga had learned Tahitian, which is quite closely related to Rarotongan, from the Raiatean mission teachers then resident on the island.

2   The Titikaveka chapel, which Ta'unga helped to build, and where he worked as a mission teacher
From William Gill, *Gems from the Coral Islands*, vol. 2 (London, 1856)

With the technical supervision of Cunningham, the first European planter on the island, Ta'unga assisted in the erection of the first coral building in Rarotonga, the Titikaveka church. Constructed with walls twenty-five feet high and three feet thick and covered with three roofs supported by ironwood columns,[17] it reflected the wish of the Titikaveka people to regain the prestige they had lost by resisting the

[16]Pitman to LMS 20.6.1843, SSL.
[17]Pitman to LMS 26.8.1841, SSL. The church was opened on 11 June 1841.

new religion for so long after the other districts had accepted it.

On 16 March 1841 Ta'unga was sent to be examined by Buzacott and Gill,[18] the missionaries in charge of the theological college,[19] and two weeks later he was admitted as a student.[20] He did well at his studies, and availed himself of every opportunity to preach in the various churches.[21] He excelled, too, in the manual arts, and a 'two-arm chair', made by him at Takamoa, was sent to the directors of the mission in London as a specimen of native skill in carpentry.[22] Some months later the missionaries decided to set apart those who volunteered for service in the heathen islands in order to 'qualify them as far as time and circumstances [would] allow for this important work'.[23] At this time the Rarotongan mission teacher Matatia, who had been working in Samoa, returned to seek a new wife, as his previous wife had died. Matatia was an eloquent preacher and an ardent evangelist and Ta'unga asked to be permitted to accompany him on his return to Samoa.[24]

[18]The Reverend Aaron Buzacott (1800-64) was missionary at Avarua from 1828 to 1857 when he retired to Sydney. For an account of his missionary work see Buzacott and Sunderland 1866. The Reverend William Gill (1813-78) was stationed at Arorangi in 1839 and left the group in 1852. See William Gill 1880. — N.G.

[19]The Rarotongan Institution (known also as Takamoa College) was founded about 1837 and has functioned continuously since then. It was Buzacott's responsibility in the early years, though during his absence in Sydney between March 1842 and January 1843 William Gill was in charge. The training course was based on that given to the missionaries at Gosport and Hoxton academies and had already been adapted for Tahiti. The theological and missionary lectures of Dr David Bogue, principal of Gosport Academy, were copied out and tuition was given in 'mechanic arts' which would be useful from a practical point of view, such as carpentry. For more detail see Buzacott and Sunderland 1866, pp. 134-5, and William Gill 1856, vol. 1, pp. 51-2. — N.G.

[20]Minutes of meeting at Avarua, 17.3.1841, SSL.

[21]Pitman, Journal, 1841, *passim*.

[22]Buzacott to LMS 6.1.1843, SSL.

[23]William Gill to LMS 17.9.1841, SSL.

[24]Pitman, Journal, 9.8.1841.

2

THE WESTWARD VOYAGE

When the mission barque *Camden* sailed from Rarotonga in March 1842, bound for Melanesia (then known in missionary circles as 'Western Polynesia'), she carried a party of Rarotongan mission teachers who were to be deposited at the various islands en route. Ta'unga was amongst them, and as they travelled from island to island he wrote the following account of their experiences:[1]

In the month of March, on the thirty-first day, in the year 1842, Mr Buzacott [Barakoti] and his wife and a party of Rarotongans departed by the mission ship *Camden*. On the second night of the month of April, on a Saturday, we reached Aitutaki where the whole lot of us went ashore.

[1]Ta'unga 1842a and b. This was the fourth Melanesian voyage of the *Camden*; the visiting party included the missionaries Slatyer, Buzacott, and Heath and two new missionaries (Turner and Nisbet) to be left on Tana. The part of this journey from Samoa onwards is described more fully in Slatyer's Journal (1842), and part appears in Turner 1861. The Reverend Thomas Slatyer (1816-54) was stationed in Samoa between 1840 and 1845 and was taking his wife to Sydney owing to her mental condition. The Reverend Thomas Heath (1797-1848), missionary in Samoa from 1836, took a senior role in the affairs of the LMS in the Pacific (in succession to John Williams) until his suicide in 1848. On this occasion Heath had been appointed to give the new missionaries 'the benefit of his experience in the difficult and perilous undertaking in which they had embarked' (Murray 1863, p. 141). The Reverend George Turner (1818-91) and the Reverend Henry Nisbet (1818-76), inseparable friends, and their wives, were left on Tana in June, but fearing they would be killed they returned to Samoa, arriving there in February 1843. Both had distinguished missionary careers and were both awarded the honorary degree of LL.D. by the University of Glasgow. The Reverend Henry Royle (1807-78) was missionary at Aitutaki from 1839 until he retired to Sydney in 1876.—N.G.

3 The *Camden*, which carried the missionaries on the voyage described
in this chapter

From Basil Mathews, *The Ships of Peace* (London, 1947)

Our hearts were overjoyed at meeting Mr Royle [Raela] and his wife and the church members of that island. We spent the Sunday there, and the Lord's Supper was celebrated. We all assembled together with the church members on Aitutaki for that communion. Mr Buzacott took the services in the morning and in the afternoon. The church was full of people. Everything we saw of that church was good. They came and looked after us well and they presented us with food and other gifts.

On the Monday morning our ship was damaged; the rudder broke. The wind was from seaward and the stern of the vessel swung on to the coral reef, causing the hinges of the rudder to break. Some of us almost met our death as we rowed to the ship. The boat was packed with people, the wind came head on, there was a strong current, the waves were enormous and our boat was almost submerged. Were it not that we were met by another of the ship's boats which had been ashore to fetch an anchor, our party would in all probability have been drowned. Some of the people transferred to the other boat and we were saved. Thus no great harm befell us except Mrs Buzacott had her fingers jammed between the two boats. Mr and Mrs Royle and their children were taken on board, and our ship set sail. We departed in great anxiety, but we soon met with fair weather and the vessel was becalmed. It just drifted about. Three days later we reached Atiu.

Mr Royle and his family went ashore accompanied by two of our party, Okotai[2] and his wife. It was evening by the time they reached the shore for they were overtaken by a storm. There was thunder, lightning and heavy rain. The boat was a long time returning from the shore and did not reach the ship until about nine o'clock that night. Only the people were able to be landed, their goods had to be left in the boat and they were all soaking wet. Next morning the wind dropped and their luggage was taken ashore. Then we found that they had not reached the village on the previous night, they had just slept at the seaside in the market house, together with the Atiu people.

On the seventh we left that island and steered straight for Samoa to get the rudder fixed properly as it was just fastened with chain. On the night of the eleventh we ran into a storm.

[2]Okotai, from the Avarua church, remained at Atiu until 1845 when he was taken to Mauke. As the people there would not receive him he was brought back to Rarotonga to teach in the Institution. He afterwards taught in Samoa and Pukapuka. — N.G.

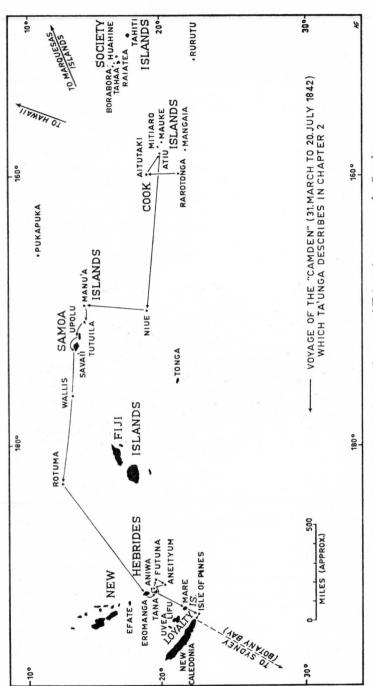

4 The South Pacific islands showing the route of Ta'unga's voyage on the *Camden*

There was thunder and lightning but by the following evening the skies were again clear. The ship sailed slowly along and we met with no harm on our voyage. God did not forsake us, He cared for us well. We did not just sit about on the ship. We prayed and sang hymns both morning and evening. We were all happy, for God was near at hand.

About Niue [Nue]

On the evening of the fifteenth day of that month we saw Arekao. Niue is the more common name for that island. The following morning we still had not reached the island owing to head winds. We encountered another storm at that time and our ship was blown off course. The next morning we again sought the island. By midday the wind had abated and the island was in sight. It was Sunday the seventeenth. We did not hold prayers in the morning because of the rain.

5 Niue canoe
From J. E. Erskine, *Journal of a Cruise among the Islands of the Western Pacific* (London, 1853)

On the Monday morning we got close to Niue and canoes came out to visit the ship. We asked about the people of that island, and were told that they had gone off to a feast. Later on many more canoes came and our ship was full of people. They came out naked. Buzacott took aside those who were only dressed in *tikoru*[3] and girded them with lengths of cotton cloth. But they did not take any notice, they just took the cloth off and some of them tied it around their heads.

[3]A coarse cloth made from the bark of the banyan tree and worn as a loin cloth.

They are a wild crowd and of strange appearance. The teeth
of the deep sea fishes are strung from their beards.

One Niue man named Beniamina[4] who was travelling on
our ship told them about God. But they asked, 'Where is
God?' He told them that God was up in heaven. They all
looked upwards and said, 'He is only the god of the ship'.
Beniamina said, 'He made the heavens and earth, and the
ocean that you see around you. And he gave His own Son
as a sacrifice so that men would be saved.' They were silent.
Buzacott gave an axe for the chief and told the people to
take it ashore to him.

That evening a man who was said to be a son of the chief
came and climbed aboard the ship with his men. He asked
for an axe and a fish hook. Those were the two things he
wanted. The missionary gave him an axe and told the people
to take it ashore. He asked us to take him back to his side
of the island, lest he be killed.[5] Then he went ashore.

We chose some people to go ashore on that island. They
were Beniamina, Ngatikiri, Paoo [Pao], Tukuau, and Tutane.
We prayed to God that their visit ashore might be a success.
The following morning when the canoes returned, the people
would not agree to the landing of the missionaries. We heard
a great deal of talk, it was very bad news. Then we thought
we would try to effect a landing. Buzacott and the captain
were going to accompany the native missionaries, but some of
the people aboard did not agree to their going. They were just
about to depart when a message arrived from ashore from
Beniamina's younger brother. This is what was said. When
the boat arrived ashore all the people in it would be killed.
They had held a meeting ashore the previous night and had
decided they would go aboard the ship and try to persuade
them to send a boat ashore. They were going to show false
affection in order to deceive us. Then they were going to
grab all our belongings. This was the reason that evil thought

[4]Beniamina (or Peniamina) had been in Samoa and had already
attempted to land on his home island in 1841. He continued as a teacher
for five years at Malua and was eventually landed at Niue in October
1846. Despite the ravages of an epidemic associated with the mission he
gained the confidence of his people and was a favourite amongst them
according to Turner in August 1848; but by 1852 he had 'acted inconsis-
tently' and left the island. — N.G.

[5]Presumably the ship had drifted round during their stay aboard. Beniamina's brother had received a hatchet the day before and because of the
jealousy this caused he felt his life to be in danger (Buzacott and Sunderland 1866, p. 160).

occurred to them: it was a sacred night,[6] and they had decided that they were going to attack. They intended postponing the battle at sea and waiting until the people came ashore.

Beniamina's younger brother told us all about it. He was in tears. 'Never, never go ashore,' he said, 'or you will die this very day.' When we heard the news we departed from that savage land and sailed on, praising God, for it was He who forewarned us of the intentions of those wicked people, so that we should not be dealt with as John Williams [Wiliamu] had been.[7] We took Beniamina's young brother with us to Samoa. He was afraid to return ashore and told us that he would be killed because he had divulged their secret to us.

About Samoa

On the twenty-third night of the month we reached Manu'a [Manuka]; it was on a Saturday. We attempted a landing in the ship's boat, but we were not successful. Next morning Buzacott and Matatia went ashore, but the rest of us spent the Sunday at sea. Buzacott took the service ashore from Psalm 144 verse 15. Matatia translated it into Samoan. Marama and Pakiao preached to us aboard the ship. The following morning the people came aboard to trade. Owing to the teachings of Nehemia this island is rich in food supplies. It is because the people responded to his teachings.[8]

The various missionaries came out to greet us and in the late afternoon Buzacott's party returned from ashore and we sailed on to Tutuila [Tutuira]. We took Masui and his wife with us from Manu'a. They had completed their term doing the work of God at Manu'a.

It was evening when we reached Tutuila and the ship entered harbour that night. We went right in and anchored at the head of the bay. The people ashore were not aware of our arrival so we fired a gun and those from the mission station came to visit us.

Buzacott and the captain went ashore to Mr Murray's

---

[6]Polynesians reckoned their auspicious occasions partly according to the phases of the moon.

[7]Williams, one of the best known of the LMS missionaries, had been clubbed to death at the island of Eromanga, New Hebrides, in November 1839. — N.G.

[8]Nehemia was a mission teacher from Rurutu in the Austral Islands. He encouraged people to extend their plantings.

[Mare][9] home but before long they came back aboard. Teava came out and greeted us all.[10] The following morning the missionaries disembarked. Ngatikiri's wife came out to fetch us and we all went ashore to Ngatikiri's place. He fed and accommodated us for four days. In the evening we went to church and the missionary, Mr Murray, told them the story of our visit to Niue.[11]

We stayed a long time in Tutuila at Mr Murray's village, Pango Pango. The church members supplied us with food. The word of God has spread widely in Tutuila.[12] On the Friday we went with Buzacott's party to the village called Leone. Five of us went, as well as Mr Slatyer [spelt by Ta'unga variously as Salatia, Seratia, Selatia] the missionary of that village. We left at daybreak and reached there early in the afternoon. If you travel round Rarotonga and go the full circle of the island, that is the same distance as the village of Leone [from Pango Pango].[13]

In the morning the drum beat for worship and all the people went to church. Mr Slatyer spoke first, giving his farewell address to the church members because he was leaving for the white man's land. It was because of the serious illness of his wife.[14] When his preaching was finished, Mr Buzacott stood up and preached. When it was all over we returned to Pango Pango with the church members, carrying

[9]The Reverend Archibald Wright Murray (1811-92) was stationed in Samoa from 1836 to 1870. He had much to do with the outstations and moved to the Loyalty Islands in 1870 and New Guinea in 1872. He returned in 1874. He wrote numerous books. — N.G.

[10]Teava, one of the most celebrated Rarotongan teachers, had been appointed an evangelist in 1832 and was stationed originally at Manono. From 1836 to 1838 he was at Falealili, Upolu. In May 1838 he moved to Tutuila and was stationed at Leone. He returned to Rarotonga in 1855. — N.G.

[11]It appears that Buzacott, not being familiar with the Samoan language, told the story to Murray who explained it to the audience in Samoan.

[12]Under Murray's evangelistic ministry a state of religious revival had been fostered. The great 'awakening' on Tutuila in 1840 attracted many converts. — N.G.

[13]The distance round Rarotonga by the ara metua, the road generally used at the time, is about fifteen miles.

[14]Mrs Slatyer's health had broken down in April 1842. According to Buzacott (1842) she was 'affected with the most distressing disease of mania'. She was to have another attack after spending about two years at Saluafata, Upolu, which caused them to leave the mission. — N.G.

Mr Slatyer's belongings. By the time we arrived the lamps were lit.[15]

The following day, which was Saturday, we went to the evening service and the next morning we assembled for communion. Great was our joy in joining the communicants of that island. They are excellent people. Buzacott explained a passage to them, as it is written in the book of John: 'Blessed are your eyes for they see, and your ears for they hear'.[16]

We sailed from that island on Tuesday. Another ship was coming into the harbour and we were sailing ahead when an accident occurred. Our ship's boat was damaged; it was broken in the middle.

Next morning there was Upolu [Kuporu] right ahead, but we did not reach it quickly owing to adverse winds. We were seven days trying to reach Upolu.[17] On the eleventh of May we anchored in Apia harbour and we all disembarked. Next morning Buzacott said farewell to us. He went away with his wife to Savaii [Avaiki], while we stayed on at Apia.

At the end of the week, on the third night, the missionaries finished their meeting at Saleimoa. We received a letter from them telling us of the decisions they had reached. Marama was to go to Manono, Pakiao to Falealili, Matatia and Tukuau were to go with Mr Macdonald [Maatono],[18] Tekori and Tutane were to go to Sapapali'i.[19] When we had finished reading that letter, we said our farewells to each other and they all went off to their various posts. We stayed on in Apia, working on the rudder. On the nineteenth the boat came to

[15]Stone oil lamps were known in ancient Polynesia; however, the missionaries were able to illuminate their churches by their own ingenious means. There were ten chandeliers in Threlkeld's church at Raiatea: 'the centre one consisted of twelve lower and six upper branches, whilst those on each side numbered ten and twelve lamps each. They were ... made of wood, carefully turned, and for lamps, thin shell of the young cocoanut, ground thinner with the rough coral rock until transparent as a horn, formed cups for the oil in which a piece of cotton was stuck upright as wick, formed a substitute for the argand lamp, and shed a mellow light' (Threlkeld 1853) . — N.G.

[16]The passage he quotes is from Matthew xiii. 16. He appears to have confused it with a similar passage from John xx. 29.

[17]The distance from Pango Pango to Upolu is only about eighty miles.

[18]The Reverend Alexander Macdonald (1813-88) resided on Rarotonga between May 1836 and February 1837, when he proceeded to Samoa. He was stationed at Savai'i until he withdrew to Auckland in 1850. In 1842 he was at Palauli. — N.G.

[19]The various Rarotongan teachers had been brought by the Camden.

take Makea to Aana.[20] By 24 May our work on the rudder was completed.

The adherents of the local church cared for us well. They supplied us with food. The word of God spread on Upolu in the village of Mr Mills [Milo].[21] Their goodness was not the same as ours. Theirs was rather strange, because they coveted articles in exchange to pay for the food they brought us. That was the true nature of their goodness!

We had a long stay there, four whole weeks. On the communion Sunday in the evening we all went on board and at dawn our ship headed for the open sea. In the month of June, on the sixth night (the day after we left) we reached the village of Matautu in Savai'i. We anchored in the harbour there and all the missionaries and the captain went ashore taking Mr Pratt's [Perati] belongings.[22] Later on they brought pigs and other food which had been purchased from inland. All the missionaries returned from ashore, the anchor was lifted, and we sailed on during the night and in the morning we reached the village of Falealupo. We took all the chairs for Mr Drummond [Taramoni] and all his belongings also.[23] We were farewelled by Marie[24] and then we sailed on. On the eighth night of the month of June we left the Samoa group entirely and sailed westward to the heathen islands. The wind

[20]Makea Davida (d. 1845) had accompanied Buzacott. 'He was anxious to see foreign lands, having been promised by Mr Williams a voyage to Sydney. The influence of such a visit it was thought, might be the means of promoting the cause of civilisation, expanding his mind, and, through him, have a beneficial effect upon his people.' Davida's father had accompanied Williams to Samoa where he was received by Malietoa, on which occasion the genealogical ties between Makea's lineage and that of Tui Aana were asserted (Buzacott and Sunderland 1866, pp. 154-5). — N.G.

[21]The Reverend William Mills (1811-76) was missionary at Apia from 1836 until he was forced to leave through ill-health in 1854. — N.G.

[22]The Reverend George Pratt (1817-94) was missionary in Samoa from 1839 to 1879 and also served in Niue, the Loyalty Islands, and New Guinea. A missionary with perception and considerable command of the language, he was primarily responsible for *A Grammar and Dictionary of the Samoan Language* published in London in 1878. — N.G.

[23]The Reverend George Drummond (1808-93) had pioneered the station at Falealupo, at the western end of Savai'i, shortly after his arrival in the group in January 1841. In 1844 he moved to the eastern end and worked with Macdonald until 1846 when he took Slatyer's station on Upolu. He remained in the group until 1872. — N.G.

[24]Marie was almost certainly the Rarotongan teacher of that name, one of the pioneer evangelists designated by Buzacott in 1832 including Teava, Matatia, and Anania (William Gill 1856, vol. 2, p. 85). — N.G.

was very favourable for that voyage. God did not treat us harshly, He helped us on our way, and He saved us through his love.

There were many of us on board. There was a group of women from Samoa, and three European missionaries who were going to Tana with their wives and their belongings and some other people who were also going to Tana with their wives. The ship was absolutely full of people.[25] It sailed straight for Rotuma.[26]

About Rotuma

In the early morning of 14 June we reached Rotuma.[27] The anchor was dropped, but there was no harbour. The water was deep even right close to the land. Buzacott and his party went inland to the house of the Samoan missionaries. It is an evil land, they have not seen the light. They will not listen to the Samoan missionaries. They simply say, 'We will not listen'.

Another problem was caused by some Europeans who advised the Rotumans to have nothing to do with the Samoans. The people of this island have an extensive know-ledge of the English language. Coconuts and yams are their staple food. Next morning Buzacott came aboard with the Samoan missionaries and the high chief as well. They were presented with gifts and returned ashore. Taomi and his wife were left there and we travelled on to Tana. We did not reach there quickly as the wind was blowing from the island. On 22 June we arrived at Eromanga [Eromango].[28] It is a

[25]Mr and Mrs Turner, Mr and Mrs Nisbet, and Mr Heath. Only Turner and Nisbet actually stayed on Tana. Heath returned on board (see p. 22). Besides the European missionaries going to Tana there were on board the ship Mr and Mrs Buzacott and their daughter, Mr and Mrs Johnston with Miss Bridge, an American lady, going to Sydney, and Slatyer and his wife, as well as the Polynesians (Slatyer 1842). — N.G.

[26]In fact the ship sailed for Wallis Island but, as it passed there at night, did not stop.

[27]The Rotuman mission had been opened in November 1839 when John Williams placed Leiataua and Sau, two teachers from Manono, on the island. Owing largely to the reports of seamen residing on and visiting the island the people had been initially prejudiced against missionaries, but they had been tolerated by one of the chiefs largely for political reasons. In 1845 the LMS missionaries removed their teachers and resigned the mission to the Wesleyans. — N.G.

[28]Slatyer (1842) gives the date of arrival as 23 June. The difference was probably due to a slip but the different concepts of time may have contributed to it. In English the word 'day' is used to refer to both

very large island, much larger than Rarotonga. It is mountainous and the sea-coast is girt with cliffs. Above the cliffs are hills and further inland are high mountains. There is absolutely no good land. Our ship sailed along close to the reef. We could see clearly the nature of the island.

We spent three days at Eromanga, and visited the spot where John Williams was killed. There is a bay running inland with a big stream.[29] It is a sandy area with high hills on one side. The anchorage is just below the stream. It is the only safe place on that island, for there are cliffs right round the rest of it. We looked at the spot where Williams died close to the hill, beside the stream. We were overcome with grief. The ship drew close in to the land because it was all deep water.

We saw the people ashore. They were just walking about. They cooked their food on top of the cliffs. We did not see a single house. There was nothing but cliffs. Mr Heath [Ite] and the captain decided to go ashore, but some of the others would not permit them to go. We just stared at that island until the middle of the third day when we left and sailed straight for Tana [1842a, pp. 2-8].

About Tana

On 25 June we sighted Tana. Because of adverse winds we were five nights tossing about between Eromanga and Tana. On the thirtieth we arrived at the harbour and the ship anchored. We thanked God for it was He who watched over us. The people came out in great numbers. They are black and quite small. Although they still have a heathen appearance it is a good island and the people treat the Samoan

the daylight hours and the twenty-four-hour period from midnight to midnight, but in its original meaning daybreak was the start of the new period. In Rarotongan, by contrast, nightfall is the beginning of the new period, and both the twenty-four-hour period and the hours of darkness are known as *po* (night). In the Rarotongan calendar, which was based on a lunar month, nights were not numbered, but each was named. In his writings, however, Ta'unga never uses the Rarotongan calendar but he writes his dates using the Rarotongan word *po* and the number of the day from the English calendar month, and sometimes its name derived from the English weekly system. In this instance he wrote 'po 22 i te marama [month] ra ko Iunu [June]...'. Although Ta'unga normally uses the English system, it is almost certain that he had no watch, and occasional differences of a day between his own and the European records may possibly be due to this. See also footnote 35.

[29]Williams River. Williams was killed on the right bank. — N.G.

missionaries well. It is a land of excessive theft. There are
ample food supplies, however, and it has no equal throughout
the islands in this respect.

We stayed there a long time taking all the belongings of
the European missionaries ashore.[30] On the Sunday we Rarotongans went ashore together with the missionaries, Messrs
Heath, Slatyer, Turner [Tana] and Nisbet [Nisabeta]. The
European missionaries did all the preaching and Mose[31]
translated into the Tana language. Large numbers of people
came to listen. They came to church with sticks and stones.

When church was over we returned to the ship. When we
got aboard the Europeans from all the ships assembled
together on our vessel. On the day of our arrival we saw
another ship already anchored in the harbour. After we
anchored yet another vessel arrived.[32] Buzacott preached to
them, and when he finished they returned to their vessels.
That evening we had communion aboard our ship and Mr
Nisbet took the service while Mr Heath distributed the bread.

The following morning we completed unloading the belongings of the missionaries. It was a lot of work. The Tana
people have a wild appearance and evil-looking faces. It is
a land of people who are black and naked. Their houses are
bad. The only clothes worn by the women are the leaves of
trees. It is a cool island.[33] That is the nature of it.

We left Mr Turner and Mr Nisbet [Nisabeta] there with
their wives, Mr Heath returned aboard, and a friend named
Kapao and the Samoans.[34] We finished our work there on

---

[30]Slatyer (1842) gives a much fuller account of this visit, including
the names of the island missionaries, one of whom was from Aniwa.
— N.G.

[31]Mose, a Samoan teacher, had been landed on Tana on 19 November
1839. — N.G.

[32]Present were the brig *Star*, Captain Ebrill, a few months later cut
out at the Isle of Pines, and a Hobart Town whaler, the *Magnet*, arrived
from Sydney on 1 July (Buzacott 1842) . — D.S.

[33]Ta'unga's visit took place in the middle of 'winter' when it can be
cool at night; but this is not always the island's 'nature'. — D.S.

[34]Ta'unga's manuscript suggests that Kapao and the Samoans came
aboard, but it could be read to mean that they stayed behind, which
Gunson assures us that they did. Kapao was a Rarotongan 'pioneer' left
with Turner and Nisbet by Buzacott. Turner records that he was a
consumptive and proved 'quite a blank' to the Tana mission. The
Samoan teachers were equally unsatisfactory. Mose was 'laid up by
ague, and alas! was *morally* as well as physically unfit', and Vaiofanga
was often ailing and had a very imperfect knowledge of the language.

9 July.[35] It was a Friday when we left that island and proceeded on our way.

That same evening we reached Aniwa [Niua], lowered a boat and deposited the Samoans Iona and his wife and Faleese, with their luggage.[36] Buzacott accompanied them ashore. That island is living in peace, and the chiefs also, and they welcomed the missionaries. The boat returned and we sailed on.

On the second day we sighted the island of Futuna [Fetuna]. It was a Sunday and we spent it at sea. That same evening the boat went ashore to fetch the missionaries. Samuela came aboard our ship.[37] The missionaries asked about the chiefs of the island, and Samuela replied, 'They have accepted the word of God'. We did not talk for long before the boat was sent to return him ashore with his wife. We had brought her with us. They went ashore with their belongings and proceeded inland.

We sailed on and in the morning we reached Aneityum [Anetomu] or Keamo. The ship anchored in the harbour there. The people of that island came, but their bodies were not clad. This was on the eleventh night of the month of July. Two men who had been left there previously as teachers had fled. It was because of their own wickedness. They had quarrelled. One had fled on another ship, and we met him at Tana. The other had gone to the far side of this island and was working for a ship's captain.[38] He had forsaken the work of God. It was a good island, the people were living in peace, and their troubles had been overcome.

The missionaries sent a message to that man and he came, telling them of his sin, and of the customs of that island.

[35]Slatyer gives Friday, 8 July (see note 28). — N.G.

[36]Iona, from Falefa, had been on Tana and was returning to Aniwa where he had first been stationed in 1841. He subsequently returned to Tana, spent a year on Lifu from May 1845 and returned to Samoa in September 1846. Faleese (born c.1826) had been one of Murray's revival converts at Pango Pango and had come as a 'pious lad' to assist the Samoan missionaries on Tana. He was to help Iona on Aniwa until the recovery of the missionary Atamu (then on Tana) from intermittent fever. — N.G.

[37]Samuela, from Falealili, Upolu, had been left with Apela by Murray in 1841. His health was very poor. The missionaries were murdered early in 1843. — N.G.

[38]This could have been Captain Ebrill of the Star; he had been there recently. — D.S.

The hearts of the missionaries were gladdened and they left
Apolo and Simeona there.[39] And that other man was also left
there to assist them with the work of God. His name was
Tavita [Davida].[40]

This was a custom of that island. If a man had four wives,
and he died, then all four wives would be brought together
to die with the husband.[41]

We departed and returned to Aniwa to buy pigs. On our
arrival the people there had already come to their decision.
They had decided to put aside all their heathen customs and
to accept the gospel. We sailed back to Tana. We did not
enter the harbour but just sent a boat in. The captain and
Mr Slatyer went ashore. When they landed the children were
all assembled within the mission compound. The missionary
was teaching them from charts. There had been a feast and
amusements and all the people had come to listen. When
the boat returned we sailed away from that island.

On 13 July our ship sailed straight for Mare [Niu Beri-
tania]. There are six other islands close to that one. We
reached there and found it in a good state. Tataio and
Taniela [Daniela], the two teachers who had stayed there,

[39]In 1845 Murray reported that Apolo, his wife and two children were
stationed at Ipeki, Aneityum. In that year Simeona, because of his
experience, was removed from Ipeki to help form a new station at
Nohos. Subsequently Simeona and his wife returned to Samoa for further
instruction at Malua, but they resumed their work on Aneityum in 1853.
According to Inglis (1890, p. 235) it was only on Aneityum that the
Rarotongan and Samoan teachers were really a success in the New
Hebrides. — N.G.

[40]The teachers Fuataiese and Tavita (or Davida) both came from
Sapapali'i and had been left at Aneityum by Murray in March 1841.
At Tana Fuataiese had given an unfavourable account of the mission
stating that the teachers had quarelled and neglected their work. Tavita,
who remained on the island, was to die of consumption about August
1843, his wife having died in the previous December or January. Turner
regarded the three teachers Tavita, Simeona, and Apolo as inadequate for
the task. They were, he insinuated, 'men who have had but little
education — who are not of tried piety — and whose wives are not
decided characters'. — N.G.

[41]The missionaries record many instances of their efforts to prevent
the strangling of a man's widows at his death — efforts often not appreci-
ated by the widows (Turner 1861, p. 93; Murray 1863, pp. 51-4). Slatyer
also reported on this custom: 'It appears that a practice exists here much
like the Suttee. — if a husband dies, his wife or wives are strangled.
—they do not know why they do it, but say that such has been the
Custom of their forefathers and that it is an essential mark of affectn.'
— N.G.

had been well treated by the people.[42] They told us all about the island. Warfare had been abolished but they would not listen to the new religion. We deposited Paoo and Zekaria there, making four of them altogether.[43]

We sailed on to the Isle of Pines [Arepaina] and dropped anchor there on the Sunday. The missionaries came out from ashore.[44] We were told that the island was living in peace but that they had not accepted the gospel. Another thing we heard was that land had been sold. Some had been acquired by Europeans.[45]

Next morning the missionaries went ashore to take presents for the resident missionaries and the chiefs. We stayed there on that island [1842b, pp. 13-15]. ⩤

[42]The Samoans Tataio from Sapapali'i and Taniela (Daniela) from Pango Pango had been placed by Murray in 1841. Tataio returned to Samoa for further instruction in 1848. Taniela died of consumption at his station in 1844. — N.G.

[43]These two Cook Island teachers were to find their own way to Lifu. Paoo, from Aitutaki, who had been on several voyages in a whaler before joining the mission, was a teacher of natural ability though with little formal instruction. Having been taken to Samoa against his will he was accepted as a replacement for a teacher at Mulifanua. He was then sent to Rarotonga for instruction in September 1841 and appointed as a 'pioneer' to the western islands in December. He spent most of his active life on Lifu where he successfully pioneered the missionary cause. See William Gill 1856, vol. 1, pp. 223-5 and 233; Macfarlane 1873, pp. 25-47. It was not until 1859 that he was joined by a European missionary, the Reverend S. Macfarlane. Zekaria was to prove a source of trouble to Paoo with whom he constantly disagreed (see p. 82). His subsequent defection and 'immoral conduct' having gravely affected the prospects of the mission, he was returned to Rarotonga in 1845. — N.G.

[44]There were four Samoan teachers resident on the island, all of whom desired to leave. Of these Taniela of Tutuila, who had been left by Heath in 1840, was so ill with dysentery that it was decided he should be taken back to Samoa to his wife and family. Noa, from Manono, who had also been left by Heath, was to be removed to New Caledonia. Considerably advanced in years, he returned to Samoa in 1845. Rangi, a Rarotongan 'pioneer', was left to assist the two remaining teachers, Taniela and Lasalo. Rangi was the only child of a widow who had been one of the first converts on Rarotonga. He and the two Samoan teachers were to die in the *Star* massacre in November. Taniela of Mulifanua, Upolu, and Lasalo of Tufulele had both been left by Heath at Eromanga in 1840, but on finding them completely deserted by the people Murray had taken them to the Isle of Pines in April 1841. Lasalo then looked 'very ill' and appeared 'consumptive'. — N.G.

[45]By this time more than a dozen European sandalwood parties had been there; one had lived there six months. — D.S.

Ta'unga's manuscript ends at this point, but he informs us in subsequent manuscripts that they were finally deposited by the mission ship not here on the Isle of Pines but nearby on the mainland of New Caledonia, in the Komwainya sub-district of a district known as Tuauru.[46] This was the last port of call on this voyage and the mission ship proceeded on to Sydney. How Ta'unga came to be the last teacher deposited is explained by him in a letter to his mentor, Pitman:

I am telling you about my visit to the heathens; all that I saw on that trip of mine, both the good and the evil. It was the year 1842 when I took leave of you. I went north in that year on the thirty-first of the month of March. It was a long trip by sea because those islands were some distance away and I was on my way to New Caledonia [Caledonia]. There were plenty of difficulties en route. Firstly, at Samoa the missionaries tried to detain me to help them in their tremendous task. I quietly asked God to inform me where He wanted me to go to do His work. I received no answer. So I informed them that I could not stay because thoughts of staying there had not entered my mind. Thus I went on to the heathens.

And when I reached an island called Tana, the two missionaries tried to make me stay there to help them with the work of God. I gave a lot of thought to the question. Even late at night I still could not sleep. I was constantly praying to God to tell me what He really wished me to do and I asked Him many times what island He wanted me to go to. But still it was not revealed to me. So I told them that it was not intended that I should stay there. I carried on to the big island of New Caledonia.[47]

---

[46]Ta'unga 1842c, 1847a, 1879.
[47]Ta'unga 1847a, p. 1.

3

ESTABLISHING THE TUAURU MISSION

Five generations before the mission ship touched the shores of the land that Cook named New Caledonia, an emigrant canoe left the island of Lifu and sailed to Kunie (the Isle of Pines). This party soon gained control over the disunited local tribes and organised a single authority structure on the island. On one occasion after four generations of succcessful control by the Lifu party, a man named Touru, who was the son of the high chief, was paying a visit to his relatives on Lifu when word reached him that his father had been killed in a battle with the people of the district of Tuauru on the south-eastern coast of the mainland of New Caledonia. Touru thereupon returned to the Isle of Pines, assumed the office of his deceased father, and organised a war party which he led on a great expedition over much of the southern portion of the mainland as far as Noumea on the western coast and Canala on the eastern.[1] *En route* they exacted vengeance on the district of Tuauru.[2]

When European visitors began to call, Touru impressed them all, traders and missionaries alike, with the degree of authority he exercised. The external features of it — such as the fact that his subjects brought him tribute and approached him on hands and knees — were by no means peculiar to him, and were indeed customary in many parts of New Caledonia as well as Polynesia. Touru's power was also more limited by custom than was apparent. Nevertheless, a strong personality and an aggressive temperament made him a man to be reckoned with.

[1]O'Reilly 1953, p. 250; Lambert 1900, p. 258 ff., says he went as far as Bourété.
[2]O'Reilly 1953, p. 250.

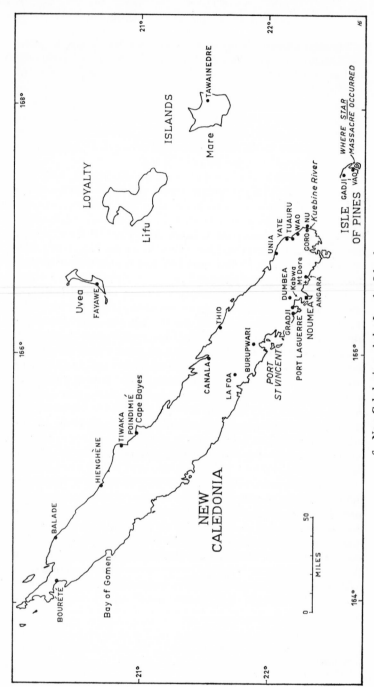

6 New Caledonia and the Loyalty Islands

The first known European contact with New Caledonia was by Captain James Cook, who skirted the east coast and anchored at Balade for a week in September 1774. D'Entre-casteaux sailed along the west coast in 1792 but was unable to land. He returned the following year and spent a month at Balade. Also in 1793 Commodore Sir John Hayes visited the island *en route* from Van Diemen's Land to India. He made only two landfalls, probably at the places now known as Port Laguerre and the Bay of Gomen.

In 1803 H.M.S. *Buffalo* put into the harbour which they named Port St Vincent to the north of Noumea, and stayed there for six weeks repairing the ship and trading with the people. La Pérouse may have called at the island too. Captain Henry had visited the Isle of Pines, and there could well have been others before the first mission voyage in 1840. The record nevertheless is of a very limited number of calls at a very limited number of points.[3]

The *Camden* sailed from Apia, Samoa, on 10 April 1840 with Heath and a number of Samoan teachers aboard to reinforce those already in Rotuma and the New Hebrides, and to visit New Caledonia. On 13 May they reached the Isle of Pines. Touru was greatly impressed by the European's property and knowledge, and was most anxious that a white man should stay on the island to instruct him in the religious arts which appeared to lie at the root of this great culture. As no European missionary was then available, however, he consented to two Samoan teachers, Taniela and Noa, being left on the island in his care.[4]

The ship sailed on, and on 18 May dropped anchor at Port St Vincent. The two Samoan teachers who had been chosen to remain there refused to go ashore for fear of being eaten, and eventually the ship sailed for Sydney with Heath vowing that he would ask for Rarotongans to establish a base on New Caledonia.[5]

The following year the *Camden* returned to New Caledonia with Mr Murray in charge of the expedition. They reached the Isle of Pines on 10 April and found that more progress had been made there than at any station they had yet visited. Murray accordingly left there Lasalo and Taniela, two Samoan teachers whom he had brought from Eromanga. He

[3]A fuller description of these early voyages is given in Shineberg 1967, chs. 3 and 4.
[4]O'Reilly 1953, p. 250.
[5]Heath 1840.

intended taking Noa to the mainland of New Caledonia but Touru, the chief of the Isle of Pines, would not consent. He was as keen to maintain his alliance with the Europeans as he was that other tribes should not. More especially was he opposed to the mission's proposal to place teachers at Tuauru, whose people recognised him as their conqueror and overlord.[6]

The other Taniela,[7] who had been on the island with Noa since the previous year, finally went with the *Camden* to the mainland. The missionaries tried to persuade a mainlander to accompany them, as he was the son of a chief at Tuauru. But the chief of the Isle of Pines, who had adopted him, would not let him go either. A Tuauru man did accompany them nevertheless, and they set sail for that part of the mainland on 14 April, reaching there the same evening. They were warmly welcomed at Tuauru, for people from there who had been to the Isle of Pines had pleaded with the mission teachers to visit them. Taniela stepped ashore, the first foreigner to do so in this part of New Caledonia, and he and a Rarotongan teacher named Mataio[8] remained there to establish a mission station which, it was hoped, would become a focal point for the evangelising of the whole country.[9]

The visitors were fortunate in that one of the sons of Uadota,[10] the chief of Tuauru, had met the mission teachers on the Isle of Pines. Uadota expressed his willingness to accept the teachers, to provide them with food and shelter, and to assist them to establish a mission station. Mataio died of illness only a few months after his arrival, and, though the mission base survived, it did not prosper.

It was on this voyage in April 1841 that the *Camden* found sandalwood at the Isle of Pines. Thereafter the isolation of the island was shattered by the visits of a large number of vessels seeking the precious cargo. The *Camden* returned to Tuauru on 20 July 1842 and deposited Noa and Taniela, both from the Isle of Pines (where the latter had been visiting), and Ta'unga, before sailing on to Sydney.

[6]Leenhardt 1953, p. 431.
[7]Both were Samoans, this one being from Falealili in Upolu whereas the one who had been at Eromanga came from Mulifanua in Upolu. —N.G.
[8]Mataio was from Buzacott's church at Avarua, Rarotonga. — N.G.
[9]Murray 1841.
[10]Sometimes spelt Uathotha or Nathotha.

Ta'unga himself recorded the main events of his stay in Tuauru, but his manuscript is unfortunately lost. Buzacott, however, collected the part covering the first three months on his way back to Rarotonga in October and translated it, and this translation is preserved.[11]

⇐This is the word relating to our arrival at Tuauru. We arrived in the month of July, on the twentieth day, the third day after the second Sabbath. On our landing we found no great evil in the land, war was abandoned, but the people still had the appearance of savages. They were however living quietly and a great number of them came to assist us in carrying our things into the house of the late Mataio. Three of us reside at Tuauru; Taniela and Noa from Samoa with myself from Rarotonga.

So we dwelt in this land, which is very, very large. They stole nothing from us and did not injure our property. We are living with one of the chiefs whose father is dead. His name is Siuaiso. Another chief also came to assist him in the ceremony of welcoming our arrival among them. This latter chief is he with whom Mataio lived; his name is Uadota[12] and he is very old. A third chief also came from a distant place, a three days' journey, and brought us a present of food. His name is Kame.[13] We are greatly rejoiced at their kindness. We are now dwelling in our house learning the language. It is a strange language, it sounds like the noise made by turkeys.

After we had been here three days the chiefs came to invite us to one of their feasts. Taniela only accompanied them, Noa and I remained that we may obtain a knowledge of the language. The place where the feast was to be held was a long distance off on the opposite side of the island. When Taniela returned he informed us of what he had seen and heard at the feast.

While the people were all met together the chief charged them to attend to two things. The first was, 'Don't let us steal lest we die, and the person who will dare to injure the teachers or their property let him be slain'. Secondly, 'Let us

[11]Ta'unga 1842c. The manuscript is presented here as translated by Buzacott in 1843, except for some changes of grammar and punctuation which appeared necessary.

[12]Guiart notes that this is a personal name still used in the area, and also in Lifu, although nowadays spelt Watota.

[13]According to Guiart this may be Dame, the name of a line of chiefs who still reside at Unia.

believe in Jehovah and cast away every strange god and let there be no war'. This was the speech of the principal chief. The feast was held on a Saturday and the next morning after his return the people assembled for worship. These people are easily persuaded and when the service was concluded I said to Taniela, 'Let you and I go to the houses of the people who have not attended worship', and we visited three houses, we were not afraid.

At the house of Tate, one of the chiefs, we saw a high house, which they told us was the place where departed spirits assemble. Only the men dare to sleep in that house. There were eight long poles standing by the entrance of that house, all adorned with birds' feathers and chickens' feathers as well. They faced upwards and when there was a breeze blowing they were wafted about. I asked, 'What is it?' And they replied that it was a sign for the spirit of a dead man. When they saw that sign it was then that they returned to live in that house. It was called the meeting house of the spirits.[14]

We turned from this and entered the house of the chief and requested him to assemble his people. He sent his son and collected them, both men and women. I requested Taniela to tell them our object in coming, and he spoke to them about Jesus, and concluding with prayer we departed. As we were going along the road another chief followed us and requested us to go to his house also and have worship there to which we consented, and made Jesus known to him and exhorted him and his household to believe, concluding with prayer.

We returned to our house and united in praising God for his goodness. Next morning we commenced school and the people all came, both old and young, and we taught them the letters. The next morning we did the same and for seven days, until, on 26 July, in the morning, the chiefs called a meeting of the people to consult about building a house for us. After the meeting one of the chiefs came to inform us of what they had done. Then we proposed that we should help them in getting the wood and to this they consented. On the twenty-seventh we commenced cutting down the wood for the house. It was the Thursday after the third Sabbath in the month of July. The people all went to assist in getting the wood.

[14]The last six sentences of this paragraph are inserted from Ta'unga 1847a, p. 2.

7   A chief's house
From Patrick O'Reilly and Jean Poirier, *Nouvelle-Calédonie* (Paris, 1959)

On the last Sabbath of this month the people all came to worship and Noa preached to them, as he knew the language, having lived a considerable time at the Isle of Pines. He exhorted them to hold fast to the word of life and not to hold it loosely. After the people had gone to their homes I said to Noa and Taniela, 'What can we do about the people who have not attended worship?' They said, 'What?' and I said, 'Let us go to them'. So we went, and we found some people at work cutting wood and we exhorted them not to work on the Sabbath lest evil overtake them and they immediately consented to leave the work and they followed us till we came to a certain place where we sat down together. Then I asked Noa to stand up and tell them about Jesus and his great love for sinners and Noa did so and they all listened.

When we had prayed together we departed and went to the house of a man whose name is Tinomumu.[15] He is a younger brother of the chiefs and we sat down in his presence without fear and he placed some food before us. I said to my two companions, 'Don't let us have any other conversation'. Then he assembled his people and Taniela gave him and his people a word of exhortation.

On our return we found the people assembled for evening service and we all exhorted them. On the Monday morning, which was the last day of the month, the people all went off again to a feast. Taniela said, 'I have a desire to go', and I said to him, 'Go, and be strong'. So he went but Noa and I remained behind. It was on 31 July.

These are a very strange kind of people. They walk about without clothing, both men and women. The latter are indeed more degraded than the former. It is, they say, what they have been accustomed to from of old. They are just the same when they sleep at night. They make a fire in their huts and then lie down and sleep by the side of it. This is a very cold land. The reason is that the mountains over-shadow it, they are so near the sea side, and because the mist and dew remain a long time on the ground.[16]

[15]Guiart observes that Ti is a collective prefix denoting respect and Mumu is a personal name in the Wecō clan of Tuauru.

[16]In his manuscript of 1879 (p. 1) he elaborates by saying 'It is a big island indeed, but comparatively few people live there. It is not a fertile land, and nothing that is planted grows well.' Ta'unga's experience was limited to the south-eastern portion of the island where settlement was restricted to a narrow littoral strip of modest fertility. Behind it lay a mountainous peridotite massif which was virtually sterile from an agricultural point of view. His own island of Rarotonga, by comparison, was fertile indeed.

The food of this land consists of bananas, taro, yams, *oi*,[17] the scrapings from the bark of the hibiscus, fruit of various kinds, with old and young coconuts, fowls and pigs. The giant taro *(kape)* is in great abundance. It is a kind that can be roasted on the fire and is not acrid, but their principal articles of food are yams and sugar cane. When they make a feast the people collect together from all sides of the island and their feasts are accompanied with dancing. This is the custom of the land. They do not now make war.

On the fourth day of the month of August the wood was obtained for our house, and during the whole time we had not neglected school. The chief and people came and requested permission to build our house and of course we consented. The people are all very kind to us and so are the chiefs, they give us food every day. Our houses are filled with yams and sugar cane, so great is their compassion for us. It was not the case a short time ago when Mataio was alive. All his and Taniela's property was expended in purchasing food but now they give it freely to us. We are thinking that in this season God has had mercy on their land, and has produced love within them, for they do our work well and with great pleasure attend to our requests. They also desire the word of God. Their conduct formerly was very different. They then paid no attention to what was said and on the Sabbath they would work, and plant, and weed, and build their houses, and there was no assembling on the Sabbath.

Mataio and Taniela were obliged to go to every house to talk with them but they were not heeded. Then Mataio died and Taniela was left alone, and the people said that Jehovah had killed Mataio. Their love and compassion for him was great and from that time onwards they were more kind to Taniela because he was left alone, and they fed him without expecting payment. So they continued up to the time of our arrival, and when I landed they showed their love by bringing me food.

On the first Sabbath after my arrival, which was 24 July, I said to Taniela, 'What is to be done supposing the people should not come to worship?' He then beat the drum and a few came but not many and I wept much and when the second Sabbath came the number was increased.

I leaned upon God and without ceasing prayed that He would make His work to grow in this land, and on the third

[17]Taro — *Colocasia esculenta,* a starchy root vegetable; *oi* — a variety of wild yam.

Sabbath a great number of people came. The people came in a body both men and women and children, and I said to Noa, 'Dear friend. I have something to say to you. If you will not be angry with me I will tell you.' He requested me to tell him. 'Well,' said I, 'I have listened to your exhortations to the people and they appear to me unsuitable. You should dwell on the great love of God to this world, and the compassion of Jesus to men, in dying for them. For I have been listening to your exhortations and they have consisted of other subjects. Do make known to them the subjects of life and death, blessing and cursing.' Then Noa stood up and spoke to them about God, His power, His great love to men, and blessings of obedience and evils of disobedience, and all the time we were leaning upon God while he was preaching.

When the service was over we went home and soon afterwards I said to Noa, 'Let you and me go to the chief's house'. When we arrived there we found a great number of people collected who informed us that the chief had been exhorting them not to do any work on the Sabbath lest they perish, but they were to remain each in his own house and do no work. Noa and I looked at each other with surprise. On entering the house he welcomed us with a loud voice, and ordered food to be set before us. We inquired of the chief if he had understood what was said in the morning and he said he understood it. We exhorted him to have faith in God that he might be saved and having prayed together Noa and I retired to our house with joy, praising God that his work was growing in the heart of the chief.

On 8 August Taniela returned from the feast which had been held at Noumea (Port St Vincent),[18] a great way off from this place and where the people are cannibals. He made known to us what had taken place at the feast. He said the people were much pleased to see him and treated him very kindly, both chiefs and people making him presents of food. While he was there when the Sabbath came he collected the people for worship and they all came and listened attentively. Toakatyu [Suakatu], one of the chiefs, said to Taniela, 'Go to Pae,[19] the war-making chief, and tell him not to cause any more war, as he is always the cause of it whenever we fight'.

[18]It is likely that Buzacott inserted Port St Vincent as Ta'unga never uses the term. Buzacott had never been to either place and, because they were in the same general area, probably assumed they were the same.

[19]Probably Pwae according to Guiart.

Taniela said that God would cause fear to grow in his heart and then he would cease to fight. He remained nine days there. We were very glad to hear such good news.

On 15 August we began teaching the children to put two letters together. Some of them soon understood how to join letters and most of them know how to read the letters, and are not forgetful, but easily learn what they are taught. Still there is no stability about them.

The land is now in a pleasing state. Two Sabbaths have passed since good began to grow in Tuauru. The people rest on the Sabbath. They do no kind of work — they do not go to fish, they do not plant, but all attend worship and attend well to instruction.[20] The first Sabbath after we landed I was very much grieved at their conduct. Some were weeding, some were fishing, some were dancing, and others were shouting and I inquired of Taniela if this had always been the case and he answered, 'It is just so, they are truly a fearless people and listen to nothing'. Then I said to Taniela and Noa, 'Let us set apart two days for prayer so that God may cause His fear to grow in their hearts and that He may bless them'. So we spent two days in prayer for this purpose and on the next Sabbath there was a great change for the better. There was an increased attendance at worship and the people came willingly and listened attentively to what was made known to them about the love of God and the compassion of Jesus. They heard and feared, because God had commenced his work in the land.[21]

On 24 August a canoe arrived from the Isle of Pines and informed us that the chief of that island had driven the teachers away. When we asked why, they said it was because the people were all dying and the chief had been asking why they died. We said, 'It is because you have not received the Word of God. Several years have now passed since the teachers came to you. Ever since they have been making known God's message to you and still you have paid no attention to it.' They then said that two ships had anchored in their harbour and the crew had asked, 'Why do you suffer those fellows from Samoa and Rarotonga to remain among you? The God of Samoa and Rarotonga is killing you and you will all be consumed'. Then we said, 'These people from

[20]Sabbatarian teaching was usually not difficult to introduce in societies which already accepted the concept of sacred days during which certain practices were forbidden. — N.G.

[21]For a statement of Ta'unga's religious beliefs see p. 6.

the ships are deceivers, why did you listen to them?' They answered that as soon as the chief heard what had been said he was very angry with the teachers and drove them away on board one of the ships.[22] They went, and took their property with them. We then inquired if there was nothing else said against the teachers and they told us that the chief was angry because the teachers had declared that there was but one God, Jehovah, who was the God of all the earth, but when those ships arrived, the foreigners told them, 'Jehovah is not our God but only the God of Samoa and Rarotonga and this God is angry with you. That is why you die away in such numbers.' Then the chief got angry and drove the teachers away. We inquired which foreigners had told them these things and they said there had been a great many. We then asked, 'Did not foreigners bring us here?' and they had nothing more to say.

In the evening we were informed that the chief of the Isle of Pines had sent the canoe with a message to the chief of Tuauru to drive us away lest his people die also. We asked what the chiefs thought about this. They said they would in no wise consent to it as their love for the teachers was very great and so was the love of all the people. They would not let us go. We then praised God for His great love to us.

On 7 October I went off to visit a distant place and as I did not know the way I hired a guide. On our way we had a large river to cross.[23] It was very deep and we swam across. It took us all the day to walk to the place. The people looked at me and were kind and asked me what I wanted. I said, 'I am come to make salvation known to you', and they inquired, 'How may we be saved?' and I said, 'Through Jesus'. Then one of them said that they had heard that the people of the Isle of Pines were all being slain by Jehovah and that he was a bad god. He spoke jeeringly. I answered that his was bad language, that Jehovah was not an evil god. His likeness was love and not anger. He was silent and I went round to all the houses to tell them that the morrow was the

[22]The brig *Star* under Captain Ebrill. As a Tahitian resident, Ebrill had some association with the LMS, transporting their teachers, and was in fact the son-in-law of the missionary Henry. He would probably have known the teachers, and would certainly have felt a more than passing responsibility for them. The teachers were obliged to leave because of the belief that they had caused the sickness. — N.G.

[23]This could have been either the Yate River (if he had travelled north) or the Kuebini River (if he had travelled south).

Sabbath and that they must not do any work, and they consented, treated me kindly and gave me food. One of them asked me to sleep in his house.

Next morning I talked to them about the true God, and they listened and said it was true. At one of the houses I visited I asked them if they knew the true God and one of them said yes he knew and that his name was Tungoe,[24] that he was the God of Noumea. I then inquired who made the heavens and earth and he was silent, for he had nothing to say. I again inquired, 'Who made you?' and he was still silent. I then made known to them that Jehovah was the true God. He alone preserves all things in existence and by him man was made. The man then said, 'We did not understand this', and when I was about to depart he said, 'Don't cast us off. Come frequently to see us.' I then said, 'This is the object for which we came to you. To make known to you the true God and salvation and you should cast away all deceitful gods.' He answered, 'We will cast them away and Jehovah alone shall be our God', and so they all said.

But the man with whom I conversed yesterday and who used bad language about Jehovah was very angry when I returned again to his house, and abused me. I approached him, however, and kindly put my hand upon his head as I was not at all afraid of him but he still appeared very angry. After sitting a little time and he not speaking I rose up and ere I departed asked him why he was so angry with me, saying 'I have great compassion for you and you ought not to be angry with me'. He followed after me and entreated me not to be angry with him for his conduct and pressed me to return to his house, and tell him and his family the object of my coming. I then returned and explained to them who that God was of whom he had yesterday spoken evil; of his great love, and of his wrath, and also of the great salvation. After that I returned to our own village, thankful to God for his kindness.

On the road I was overtaken by a chief who invited me to his house saying he had been waiting for me. I found all his family assembled. He placed some food before me. I exhorted him and all his house to attend to the word of life. He answered, 'I will believe in God that I may be saved', and added, 'I will abandon my old gods'. This I encouraged him

[24]Guiart identifies this with Tonggo, the name of the divinity in the Dubea language of the south-west coast.

to do, assuring him that if he were sincere Jehovah would save him. The name of this chief is Teuvea.[25] When I arrived I made known what had happened to my brethren and we all united in praising God. I was then come to the eighth of October.   ⇐

This concludes Buzacott's translation of the manuscript describing Ta'unga's first three months' stay on the island. In a later manuscript, however, he gives the following additional information, principally on the internal workings of the new mission:[26]

⇐I asked Noa and Taniela about the progress made during their stay on the Isle of Pines and they told me that our religion had no hold there. So I asked them, 'Which day did you set aside for praying to God so that He would give you good fortune?' They replied, 'None'. I said to them, 'Oh, my friends. This is my advice to you. This work will not progress if we sit and do nothing. Rather by asking shall we receive. This work is not for man alone for him to do nothing. It is God's work so let us ask God to give us good fortune. It is only then that the work will progress. Let us devise ways in which goodness shall spread quickly throughout the land.' They both agreed and we set aside the fourth night and Friday also when we would pray for good fortune. We prayed every evening and also on the day we had set aside specially for it. Never did we cease praying to God to bless that island.

A few people began being friendly towards me but not to those two Samoans because they were bad tempered and the people were not attracted to them.[27] They came to me alone and I took good care of them. The Samoans were jealous because the people came to me. They were angry with me, saying, 'Why do the people come to you only and not to us?' And I said, 'Brothers, I do not know'. They replied, 'Perhaps

[25]Te is a collective prefix. Uvea might very well indicate a Polynesian ancestry. Guiart states that a clan named Te Wea at Unia still claims Polynesian ancestry.

[26]Ta'unga 1847a, pp. 2-5.

[27]The Rarotongan teachers regarded themselves as senior to the Samoans in the mission field, having played a vital role in the evangelisation of Samoa. The Samoans, on the other hand, regarded themselves as a more cultured people and resented the Rarotongans. The European missionaries, too, had prejudices and Buzacott referred to the Samoans as 'the French of the South Seas' (Buzacott and Sunderland 1866, p. 124) . — N.G.

you went and told them not to come to us?' I said to them,
'Let not such words be heard between us. I did not do such a
thing. I only know of one thing, and that is my great joy in
the way that God has sought to bring the people close to us.'
But they still persisted with their accusation and I said to
them, 'Do not persist. Go and ask the people about it. Let's
put an end to this argument.'

On the second Sabbath more people came to the service
and when prayers were finished I returned to the home of
the chief whom I visited first and when I arrived there was
a gathering of people at his home. I said, 'Why are there
many people here?' and someone replied that the chief had
spoken to them saying, 'Do not work on Sunday. Do not go
fishing on Sunday. Do not weed, play or speak evil on Sunday,
and let us gather our food on Saturday ready for Sunday.
Sunday must be a sacred day.'

When I heard those words, my joy was great. As soon as
I entered, the chief told me about these things. I praised God
for having sown the seed of those good thoughts in that
chief's mind. I stayed at that chief's house and when the drum
was sounded for evening worship he and I went to prayers.
I told both my friends about this and we praised God for
taking that chief into His hands. His name was Uaroku.[28]

We continued doing this every Sunday and every month.
We never failed. And when I knew the language of that
island well, we said to ourselves, 'It is not right that we
should stay in one place. We should go to other places too,
then maybe the people will receive the word of God.' But
they would not agree to this.

One Saturday I said to them, 'You take the service here,
I shall spend this Sunday at Nao.[29] When I arrived there it
was evening for I had left in the late morning. I went and
greeted the chief Kapea [Kapia] at his house. He welcomed
me and fed me as Uadota had done. He asked about all the
new things which had been started at our village and I told
him. He said, 'Is tomorrow a sacred day?' and I said, 'Yes,
how did you know?' He said someone from our village had
told him about it. 'We have been observing this for two
Sundays now', he said. My heart was gladdened for God had

[28]According to Guiart Warëku is a personal name in the Wecō clan
of Tuauru.
[29]Guiart suggests that this may be either the island now known as
Nu (or Nau) off the river Kuebini (Kubigny), or the river itself, the
traditional name of which is Nowe.

chosen him first. 'How did you observe that day?' I asked;
and he told me, 'We did not work, we did not go fishing,
neither did we do the various things of the body. We did
nothing on that day for we did not know how to pray. We
did nothing but eat.' Those were the words of that chief.

The next morning I asked the chief, 'Have you many
followers?' and he said that there were many. I asked him to
gather all his people together so that I could see them. They
were collected from all the households and they gathered at
the chief's house. They all stared at me for that was the
first time they had seen a person from somewhere else. I said
to the chief, 'Would you agree for me to speak to you and
your people?' And he agreed, so I preached about what God
was like and His creation of the first man in this world. I
spoke about Jehovah, who created that first man; the sinning
of that man and the death of mankind because of that sin; also
about God's great love in giving His Son to absolve that sin
so that all men should live.

When that service was over they all returned home and I
said to the chief that I would go too. He requested me not to
go too soon but I refused. He asked if I would return to
them on the following Sunday and I agreed. So I returned
to our village which was some distance away. It was my first
visit to this other place. They formed a village and I often
went there on Sundays and the chief became a devoted
convert. After his passing, all this goodness was carried on by
his son who succeeded him. He clung tenaciously to righteousness and never let go. He was a good chief too. His name
was Dame.[30]

Soon afterwards we built our church. We first began our
prayers in our own house but there was not enough room.
That was why we built our church. It was the chief who
suggested that we should build it and the people brought the
timber and the pandanus. I organised the construction.[31]   ❦

[30]According to Guiart, Dame was one of the principal warring chiefs
of the area, oral tradition recording that he agreed not to interfere when
the Isle of Pines people came to make war on Tuauru.

[31]We have no information on the style of the building but Polynesian
teachers frequently imported building styles from their home islands
in constructing churches. Many churches built under indigenous supervision incorporated traditional fertility motifs in the woodcarving to
the embarrassment of the missionaries. — N.G.

4

THE *STAR* MASSACRE

No sooner had the *Camden* reached Sydney than another
vessel arrived there with the news that the high chief of the
Isle of Pines had 'ordered the teachers all to leave, saying that
the God of Samoa and Rarotonga was destroying all his
people'. He had told them to go and 'take their God with
them'.[1] Throughout the history of missionary contact missionaries and teachers were frequently accused of bringing disease
or deliberately praying for death. All too ready to blame
traders and visitors for introducing and spreading plagues and
venereal disease, they did not always realise their own lethal
role in carrying influenza, measles, and even parasites. The
chief was quite possibly right in his diagnosis that the
epidemic then raging on his island and killing his people
was brought by the teachers, though they themselves seemed
unaware of such a possibility.

The ship accordingly hastened her departure from Sydney
and returned to New Caledonia. Just two days before her
arrival at the Isle of Pines the teachers had fled with Captain
Ebrill of the brig *Star*. The chief refused to see the
missionaries and after two days' fruitless stay they sailed on
to Tuauru where they were gratified to find that the people
'appeared greatly to love and respect their teachers'. The
people of Tuauru were in the course of building a house for
the teachers to serve as a joint dwelling and chapel. During
the three months since he had landed, Ta'unga had applied
himself to learning the local language, and Buzacott found
him able to converse freely with the people. He had written a
considerable vocabulary of their language with translations
into Rarotongan which Buzacott took away with the intention

[1]Buzacott to LMS 29.9.1842, SSL.

of preparing some vernacular tracts.[2] With Ta'unga's journal as related in Chapter 3 on board,[3] the *Camden* tacked away eastward, back to Polynesia.

Ta'unga has left us the following account of the return of the mission ship and of the ominous turn of events which followed its departure:[4]

⇜The next morning, which was Monday, a ship was sighted and we thought it was another ship but when a boat came ashore I realised that it was Buzacott's ship and that the boat was our own. I greeted them and when they came up to our house, all the people gathered together. Buzacott exhorted them to hold fast to the good that they had achieved, remaining steadfast until death. I interpreted this to them in their own language. The captain told them, 'Be steadfast. I myself will bring you a European pastor.' We all prayed and when it was over we went on board the ship together with three of the chiefs. Buzacott treated them well by giving them articles to keep.

Buzacott told me: 'Your enemies are close at hand and I felt sorry for you in case you were ill-treated during your stay on this island'. He gave me encouragement and he left Teura[5] as a companion for me, taking Taniela back to Samoa. So that ship left. We stayed on and after a while we thatched our house and when it was completed we began teaching and all the people came to the lessons. Buzacott also told me that the two teachers at the Isle of Pines had been chased away and that was why they called to see us. That was the first such news we had heard.

Not long afterwards a canoe came from the Isle of Pines to fetch the two chiefs of Tuauru [Duauru] to attend a feast. They refused to go. So the canoe returned. Later on two other canoes came to get the chiefs and this time they agreed

[2]Buzacott to LMS 4.1.1843, SSL.

[3]Ta'unga 1842c.

[4]Ta'unga 1847a, Supplementary material from his manuscript of 1846b has been incorporated into the 1847 text where it elaborates or clarifies that manuscript. Information in the later manuscript which merely repeated what had already been said in the earlier one has been omitted. The relevant source is identified by the insertion of the date and page of the text in square brackets at the end of each extract. Another version of the story, as told to him by Ta'unga and Noa, appears in Turner 1861, pp. 412-16.

[5]Teura was 'a pious young man' from Rarotonga. He died of consumption in July 1844. — N.G.

to go. One chief came to me saying, 'Would you be agreeable
to accompanying us all?' But I refused. They went and slept
on another part of the island and at daylight they set sail
but they were soon becalmed. So they slept ashore on an
island [1847a, p. 6]. One night they saw a strange sight. It
was a light which glowed red in the sky and the people said:
'What is happening on the Isle of Pines?' [1846b, p. 51]. The
party arrived there at daylight on 3 November 1842.

They landed at Gadji [Caji],[6] but saw no one [1847a,
pp. 6-7]. When they reached a certain part of the island they
saw some women just sitting about [1846b, p. 52]. They
asked, 'Where are the chief and his people?' The women
replied, 'They have gone to Vao. Yesterday, a ship's crew was
massacred and the mission teachers were killed also. The
chief is there with his family, gathering all the things from
the ship.' Everyone on the ship, including Captain Ebrill
[Ebera] and the two teachers, was dead. When they asked the
reason for the murder they were told that it was because of
the chief's wickedness [1847a, p. 7].

Those who were killed on the ship were six Europeans,
two men from Huahine [Huhaine], two Mangaians, one
Aitutakian, one from the Marquesas [Makuisa], three
missionaries, one man from Maui (Hawaii) and the son of
Mr Henry [Heneri].[7] There were seventeen of them all
together. Among the dead were Taniela, Lasalo [Lazaro],
Rangi, and another named Rengora. Every one of them died
[1846b, p. 52].

The Tuauru party sent a messenger to get the chief but
he would not come immediately because he had so much to
do in connection with the ship. So they slept at Gadji and the
next morning the chief came. Matuku [Mathuku] was his
name.[8] Uadota asked him, 'Why did you kill those Europeans?
What did the Europeans take from your island? Did they ill-
treat you and your people? Did our ancestors witness all these
modern things that we see nowadays? They passed on without
ever seeing Europeans and all the various things that we see

[6]Gadji was the seat of the local paramount chieftainship.

[7]This was Ebrill's nephew, William Henry, eldest son of Captain
Samuel Pinder Henry who had also traded for sandalwood in the area,
and grandson of the Reverend William Henry, LMS missionary in Tahiti.
He would have been aged about twenty. — N.G.

[8]Guiart points out that Matuku is not a personal name, but a term
of respect for a high chief. He gives Madoku as the correct modern
spelling. The chief referred to here has been identified by Shineberg
as Touru.

8   The palisaded dwelling of Matuku at Gadji
From O'Reilly and Poirier, *Nouvelle-Calédonie*

now [1847a, p. 7]. It is only our generation which has had
this privilege [1846b, p. 52]. You must be a silly fool.' And
when that chief heard what the chief of Tuauru said he
became angry indeed and gave the visitors no food to eat.
Neither were they given a share of the things from the
plundered ship. But they stayed on nevertheless.

One day, however, a feast was arranged and they all
gathered together at one spot. Then Matuku spoke to Uadota
saying, 'You must kill the two teachers at Tuauru also. Do
not leave them or we shall all die. They are the cause of all the
deaths in these islands.' Uadota said to him, 'I shall not kill
for I have a compassionate heart. I am not like you. You have
killed all yours but I shall not kill mine.' Matuku was
insistent. That evening he placed an axe in the hands of the
chief from Tuauru saying, 'Go and kill the two teachers in
Tuauru. I know for sure that they are the cause of all the
deaths in our country.' Uadota replied, 'Friend, I shall not
do it, lest I myself should die together with all my people.'
But he accepted the axe and decided to tell his high chief
(who was also named Uadota) as he knew that he would not
consent to the request either.

One day, that chief from Tuauru sent some messengers,
who had accompanied him on his trip, to tell the high chief

of that request. They brought the axe to the chief with whom I was living saying, 'Uadota has commanded that you continue following the word of God. Do not cast it aside, for the Isle of Pines has been overwhelmed by death. Only a few remain alive.[9] Captain Ebrill's ship has been plundered and the people on it murdered. The two teachers are also dead and the chief there has sent you this axe to kill our teachers for this is a sacred axe. He has requested that you kill them immediately so that we shall know that it has been done before we return.'

The chief asked, 'Why did you bring me such dreadful news. I shall never behave like that.' So he took the axe and came to tell me about the things that Uadota had sent to show his sympathy for my friends who had been killed at the Isle of Pines. He laid them before me saying, 'Oh Ta'unga', calling my name while tears streamed down his face, 'Let this be a secret between you and me. Just you and me. Do not tell anyone.' And I assured him that I wouldn't tell a soul. So he spread out a *tapa* cloth and told me, 'This cloth was sent by Uadota as a sign of his compassion for your murdered friends. He is very sorry for you, because you all come from the same island.

'And I wish to tell you that the chief of the Isle of Pines is anxious that you be killed and that the word of God be completely wiped out from the whole country. Here is the axe which he sent me, to kill you and your two friends.' With that he put the axe into my hands and when I looked at it, I saw that there was still blood on it, but it was dry. It was the very axe which had been used to kill the other two teachers and that was why it was sent for killing us.

When I heard his words I asked him, 'Do you agree with all this?' and he replied, 'I shall never agree.' Then he told me that the chief had also said that if he did not kill me, then he and his followers were coming over to kill me themselves. So I said to him, 'That is all right. It is good that we should die in the name of our chief, Jesus the Messiah, but it would be wrong for us to die just for having caused trouble between the chiefs of this island. We do not wish that' [1847a, pp. 7-9]. The chief wept when he heard our words, and said, 'If you are killed then I will be killed also'. We replied, 'O chief, that is very true. But if you die together with us

---

[9]Ta'unga (1846b, p. 53) mentions that Uadota particularly requested Ta'unga to pray to God to save him and his family from death.

48 THE WORKS OF TA'UNGA

it will not do you any good. But if you die having faith in
Jesus, then death will be a blessing for you.'
Uadota went away weeping. I spoke to Noa and Teura
saying, 'Friends. What has been said is very true. We know
that the chief is weeping. It is true that we are about to die
but let us not be troubled, for ours is not a pointless death.
We came here through the great love of Jesus, that all people
may be saved. Let us recall that Jesus said, "Fear not them
which kill the body".[10] It is worth nothing to them. Let us
fear God. Let us pray to God. Let us be diligent in prayer
and He will take away our troubles' [1846b, p. 53].
I asked Uadota, 'Why are we to be killed?' And he
answered, 'Because of all the deaths which have occurred
throughout these islands. Matuku puts the blame on you, for
this is the first time that deaths like this have occurred.' I said
to him, 'And are we the cause of the deaths?' and he replied,
'Who knows?' I asked him what he thought. 'Why did you
not agree with Matuku's demand? Both of you are chiefs.'
He replied: 'He is chief on his own island. He belongs to a
different hierarchy. I am chief of my own island. Mine is an
independent authority [1847a, p. 9]. One chief cannot just
come and kill the people of another chief. Great trouble
would ensue if that happened [1846b, p. 53]. I shall not
dispense with the word of God, neither will I let you be
killed. Not till I myself die will you die also.' I said to him,
'What sins have you committed that you should be killed?
You have not done wrong. It is we who have sinned. That is
why we are to die.' He replied, 'I do not wish you to die
before my eyes for you hold the keys to my desire to know
the word of God.' When we heard the chief's sentiments we
praised God for His great goodness in delivering us from
death. So these messengers returned having been refused. The
chief gathered all the people together and I encouraged them
all to continue their prayers and to heed the word of God
[1847a, pp. 9-10].
Some time went by before Uadota returned from the Isle
of Pines and told us how the two teachers had been slain
together with Captain Ebrill and all the crew of the ship.
Not one remained alive. Ueiji, assisted by Ienikare, Kiamo,
Niuthu, Kadei, Uima and all their followers murdered those
on the ship. Those from Lifu were Uadengeji, Uaima and
their followers, and those from Tuauru were Kade, Uaraui,

[10]Matthew x. 28.

Uadengeji,[11] Jinja, Nama and their followers. The two chiefs from Unia, Ukupore and Ngao[12] and their followers, were also responsible for the massacre of those on the ship. They killed them on the second night of the month of November, in the year 1842, and it was on the third night that the two teachers were killed. He told us that the ship had been burnt and that many of the local inhabitants had died.

Deaths like this had never occurred in former times. This is the way it happened. When the murderers brought things ashore they collapsed at the spot where those things were deposited. Those who kidnapped the teachers died. A son of the chief died and all the people who lived at the place where those things from the ship were gathered died too. It was a most amazing death. The women and children died too, and the whole island stank because nobody was buried. Anyway, who was there to dig the holes? And who was there to carry the dead? Who was able to walk? Those who remained alive tried to bury the dead but death came upon them also. Thus they were abandoned and the ground stank. The people just left everything and did nothing at all. There was no sympathy for loved sons and loved daughters. A father took no notice of the death of a son, neither did the mother see the death of a daughter. Similarly with friends. They just died hither and thither, for death came quickly upon the people. That was what the chief told us.

I asked him, 'What wrong was committed to cause the slaying of the ship's crew and the teachers?' And he replied, 'It was because of the epidemic. They said that the gods of Samoa and Rarotonga and also the Europeans had brought death to them. That is why they retaliated.' There was another thing: it was to avenge the assault on the chief's sons by the Europeans. They went to barter things on the ship and they took sandalwood to pay for what they wanted. When they got on board they sold their sandalwood but they did not get a fair price for it. The Europeans got angry and seized the sandalwood and stowed it in the hold. But those who owned the sandalwood fetched it back. The Europeans became incensed and beat them up. Some were made unconscious and others were bashed with timber. Some were

[11]Guiart considers that Uaraui and Uadengeji were probably Mare island people who were living at Tuauru.

[12]Ukupore is identified by Guiart as Ukapwere (a man of the Atinua clan of Unia) and Ngao as Nyau (another clan from Unia).

slashed with swords and others were bruised with punching. Others again were shot in the arms.

When they came ashore exhausted and the chief saw them, he was furious, and asked, 'Wasn't there a mission teacher on the ship?' They replied, 'Lasalo[13] is still on the ship but he didn't attempt to stop the fighting'. So the chief went to the house of the two teachers and called out, 'Where's Lasalo?' They replied, 'He's on the ship'. The chief said, 'Why didn't he restrain the Europeans? My family was nearly killed by them. Why is it that he himself has fled? Why do you ill-treat me and my family? Why do you side with the Europeans. Aren't I your master? If I got angry and killed you, would the Europeans come and save you from my hands? You certainly are troublemakers.'

As soon as he was gone they said to one another, 'Let us flee to the ship'. So they went on board and told Lasalo what had happened. They decided to stay on board and to leave the island. They told Mr Ebrill, the captain, about it and he agreed to return them to Samoa.

That same night the captain sent two boats ashore secretly to collect the teachers' belongings. It was dead of night when they landed. The teachers loaded all their belongings into the boats. They were not seen by the people on the island.

At dawn the chief came to check. But when he reached the house there was no one in it. Neither were there any belongings left. The reason for the chief's visit was that he regretted the way he had spoken to the teachers and he came to bring them an offering. Then the chief said to himself, 'Ah, these people are holding a grudge against me'. So he sent his family on board the ship to get the teachers, but they refused to come. They returned ashore and told the chief and he sent a different canoe with a son of his who was also a man of rank. So he went on board and said to them, 'Come. The chief weeps for you all. Why did you listen to his talk. It is because he knows you well that he spoke like that. He searches in vain for the cause of your sudden departure. Did he ill-treat you when you stayed with him? Did he steal any of your things? Thus he seeks the reason for your going away.'

Lasalo called out to them, 'Return to the shore. We are not coming back. Your father ill-treated us.' Kadei, one of the chief's sons, asked, 'Did our father beat you? He treated you kindly. He fed you from the day you came. You are the

[13]Lasalo: see Chapter 2, n. 44.

leaders of this island. Don't you feel sorry for our father, who treated you so well? You really are a queer crowd.' But Lasalo called out, 'Hurry ashore. The Europeans are angry with you.' So they went ashore, but it was when they were going ashore that the Europeans made faces at them and in retaliation they showed their backsides to the Europeans who became angry and shot at them. The canoe was holed by bullets and it sank. They swam ashore and told their father about it and he wept, saying, 'Leave it for the time being until their anger has abated. Then we'll go and try again.'

On the third night, that ship sailed and anchored off another part of the island and when the chief heard about it he gathered some tribute and again sent for the teachers. He also sent payment to the captain so that he would not detain the teachers.

So they boarded the ship and when the teachers saw them, they disappeared below to hide. When the Europeans saw that the teachers had hidden they got up and prepared to throw those from ashore into the sea. They tried to scare them with swords and guns. They took the offerings of food and then pushed the men overboard. Some swam ashore, others went back by canoe. It was at this last group's departure that the Europeans shot at them with guns, hitting the stern of the canoe and lodging a bullet in the thigh of the chief's son. The head of another had been wounded by a sword, while yet another had been punched when on board the ship. And again they shot and one of them was wounded in the hand. So they jumped overboard and abandoned the canoe. When they reached the shore they told the chief and he was furious. He decided to fight and said that they would attack next day. He organised three groups for the fight, but the following morning the ship was gone so no battle took place.

In October Buzacott and the others returned from Sydney [Setani], that is from Botany Bay [Panipe]. When they reached the Isle of Pines the teachers were not there. Someone was sent ashore to find out, but he was told that the teachers had gone. So they came on to New Caledonia to see whether they were living with us. But they were not.

On the first day of November, Captain Ebrill's ship came back. They had been to Tana and Aneityum [Anatomo] and had returned from there. The ship anchored at Vao, on the other side of the Isle of Pines, and when the people found that it was the very ship which was carrying the teachers they reported it to the chief, and when his family heard about it they prepared to attack.

This is the plan they followed in capturing that ship. They all went on board with their weapons of war. But the chief was not aware that they had done this. Perhaps they remembered their old methods of fighting during the visit of that ship, for when they got on board they distributed the weapons to each one, and one of them stood close to each European, but the Europeans were not aware of the ruse. The captain was standing by the door which led below deck. An Isle of Pines man called Niuthu went up to him saying, 'Come and sharpen my axe'. Mr Ebrill came, took the axe from the man's hands, and placed it on the grindstone, while the same man turned the handle. When it was finished the captain said to him, 'Is it good?' and he replied, 'Very good'. So he placed the axe into the man's hands and immediately after he had taken it, he slashed at Captain Ebrill, knocking him over.

When the others saw that the captain had been killed they attacked the rest of the people on the ship. Those who were left fled below. They were dragged out and bashed with pieces of sandalwood, breaking their legs and their arms. Some ran and climbed up the masts. The masts were chopped until they crashed with all those people on them. That is how they were killed. But they kept the two teachers and Mr Henry's [Hanere] son alive and they led them to the chief. When they reached a certain road, they met a son of the chief who offered his left hand saying, 'Greetings'. Mr Henry's son replied, 'Greetings'. Instantly he was chopped dead with the axe. Next they attacked the two teachers. Lasalo, however, did not die straight away. He had been struck, but was not yet dead. He ran towards the chief who called out, 'Come, come quickly'. He prostrated himself before the chief saying, 'Oh, Matuku, have you no sympathy for us?' And the chief replied, 'I have some feeling for you'. Again he called out, 'Have you no pity for us?' And the chief replied, 'Yes. A bit.'

The chief then stood up and moved aside and another man stepped forward to kill Lasalo but he ran into the sea and they shoved him under the water. Still he survived. Again he was pushed under but even then he would not die. His body was badly mutilated by spears and stones and he was left to float about in the sea until he was washed ashore on an islet. He climbed the rocky shore and when the people realised that he was not dead, they paddled over in a canoe. He had just finished praying when they reached him and they seized him and flung him from the rocks. So he died and his body was brought to the mainland.

I said to him, 'What happened to the body? Did they eat it?' and he replied, 'They intended eating it but some would not agree. The chief had ordered that it should be eaten but Soko, who was one of his younger brothers, forbade it.' It was Soko who said, 'Let us not eat him or we shall die. This is what I think, bury him.' Then the chief agreed. The bodies were strewn along the paths near the shore, and there they were left, including those of the two teachers. That night some were stolen by thieves and were cooked and eaten. But when they finished eating death came to all those thieves. Death followed in this place and that place. Even when a woman went to live with a man from a different place, they were pursued by death and even their families died. There were no people left in that place and all their lands were taken by the chief. That was what Uadota told me.

When we heard that story, we all wept. The first time we had heard it we didn't believe it for we thought it was just a lie. But now we knew it was true that they were all dead. After our weeping, we thanked God for saving us for we nearly died too. It was His love that saved us. We gathered together in a room and decided, 'Let us not tire. We won't let the Devil wipe out the Word of God. Let us not look at the dead. They are dead. We won't let that enfeeble our hearts for if He intends to end us all in death then that is good. Ah, He has saved us to do His work.' And so we took courage, believing in God and carrying on with his work in those troublous times. Evil was growing fast and men were planning to kill us, but this saying of Jesus served to strengthen us: 'And I shall be with you always, even unto the end of this world. Amen.'

The chief of the Isle of Pines said to the chief of Tuauru, 'Do not show favour to those men from Rarotonga and Samoa. They are evil priests and they will kill us all. Kill them or else just chase them away. If you do not do it, I myself will come over and kill them. Many Europeans have said to me, "Do not believe them. The Europeans have no Jehovah. Jehovah comes from Rarotonga and Samoa. He is a man-eating god. That is why you are overcome by death. As for us we do not die, because we do not have the God, Jehovah".' Uadota listened to the speech of the chief of the

Isle of Pines and he brought the news to us. 'These are deceitful words', we told him. 'Do not listen. Wasn't it the Europeans who brought us here? Wasn't it a European ship that brought us ashore here. What country has not heard about Jehovah, except those which have not yet been reached?'

Then all the people came to church regularly, without neglect. They did not listen to that chief's words. And it was like that every Sunday [1847a, pp. 12-20].   ⇐

5

THE YATE INCIDENT [1]

⇐I went to Yate [Adi] one Sunday morning as our work had been shared that day. Noa went to Wakun, Teura stayed in our village, and I went to Yate. A boy showed me the road and when he reached the boundary of the district he said, 'I am going back'. I replied, 'Yes, go back, lest you be killed'.

This was the reason he went back. It was a different tribe which was always fighting against our village. That was why he was frightened. I went on my way all by myself. About a mile and a half later I heard the tramping of feet. I glanced back and saw two 'man-stealers' following me. I waited until they reached me and I asked, 'Where do you come from?' They replied, 'We come from our village' [i.e. the same village as Ta'unga]. 'And where are you going?' I asked. They replied, 'We are going to Yate'.

They were besmeared with charcoal from head to foot. Their faces were completely covered. Only their teeth and the whites of their eyes stood out clearly. It was impossible to see who they were. They asked me where I was going. I told them that I was going to Yate and they said, 'Let us go together'.[2] I said, 'You two go on'. But they persisted that

---

[1]This account is taken from Ta'unga 1879, pp. 32-8. Although he tells it as a single incident, two much shorter accounts in the 1847a manuscript (pp. 10 and 21-2) suggest that it may in fact have been two separate incidents. At p. 10 he tells how he escaped from the plot to kill him on his way to Yate by going to the bush to relieve himself and then fleeing home. At p. 22 he tells of his being attacked with spears while on his way home from Uao (which place we have not located) and of his escape by swimming across the inlet. It is likely that in the intervening thirty-two years the two incidents became compounded in his mind.

[2]Ta'unga (1847a, p. 10) says he asked them the whereabouts of the chief named Thoku (Guiart points out that *doku* or *thoku* means chief,

we should all go along together. So we did. One of them was
in front, the other behind, and me in the middle, until we
came to an inlet which went right into the mountains. The
road curved away inland. The distance from the inlet to the
foot of the mountains was probably two and a half miles.
The path inland from the sea followed the inlet.

The path went right up over the ridge and descended a
steep incline, then it climbed again over another ridge, and
then I leapt into a stream. We must have covered five miles
before we reached the stream. One of them stood on one
bank and the other stood on the other. I was down in the
water, drinking. Suddenly I heard them talking in the Gradji
or Karatyi [Karrachi] language.[3] One said, 'What shall we do?'
and the other replied 'Kill him'. But his companion said
'Don't be in too much of a hurry'. They thought I did not
understand the Gradji language. When I heard what they
said I stood up in the water and called out, 'I want to go
into the bush to relieve myself'. So I went downstream and
when I reached a bend near the path whence we came, they
could not see me. So I clambered up the path and started
running for the village.

As soon as I reached the top of the ridge they saw me and
began to chase me. When I reached the bottom of the valley,
they were on top of the ridge and when I got to the top of
the next ridge they were just descending into the valley.

I ran along the ridge and when I reached the inlet I
jumped into it and began crossing to the other bank. They
threw two spears at me in the water. One went over my head
and landed in front of me, while the other just missed my
ear.

A wave carried me to the other side of the inlet and I
rested on a rock there. They jumped into the water too, but
they didn't quite make this bank for the current swept them
back into the inlet. They persisted, however, and finally
reached this side, exhausted. I ran on again with them in
pursuit.

When I reached the top of another ridge I slowed down.
Again they threw their spears but I managed to dodge them.
One passed my side and the other went under my feet,

---

but that the word was also used as a personal name) and they said
they would show him.

[3]This language was spoken, according to Guiart, on the northern side
of the mouth of the Dumbea River.

landing ahead of me. I picked them up and when they saw
I had them in my hands they turned back.[4]

I returned to the village and, on reaching our house, I
collapsed on the mat. Before long the people began gathering
for the evening service and after the service my two friends,
Noa and Teura, came. They thought I was sick because I did
not speak for a long time. After their persistent questioning
I told them and they wept. We thanked God for saving us
from the hands of the heathens.

At sundown, the chief came to ask, 'Why didn't you come
to church? Were you ill?' So I told him all about the day's
happenings and he replied, 'You silly man. Didn't I tell you
not to go in case you met with thieves along the road? You
were very nearly killed.' The chief added that the two men
were from Kabwa [Kampa][5] or perhaps from Thio [Anchio].
He returned to his house and after our prayer we went to
sleep.

The next morning, I went to Kae's house for he was sick.
I sat down beside him and greeted him. Then he spoke,
saying, 'Did you know about the battle last night?' and I
asked, 'Who did the fighting?' He replied, 'Our district', and
I told him that I did not know about it.

He told me that the fight had started soon after the chief had
returned from his visit to me. They went to pursue the two
men who had chased me. They caught up with them in a
cave at Burupwari [Purupare]. A fire was burning inside.
They blocked the entrance to the cave. One man was killed
and the other was kept alive. I asked, 'How many were there?'
'Only two', he replied. So I asked again, 'What happened to
them?' and he replied, 'They carried the dead man back and
the other was led back. They are at Dikadu's place where all
the chiefs are assembled with the rest of the warriors. The
ovens are lit ready to cook the two men.'

I stood up and ran inland through the bush until I reached
Dikadu's house. When I looked I saw the live man all trussed
up to the post of the cook house, but the other had already
been cut up but not yet divided out. The live man was just
looking at me and when I realised that it was the very man
who had been behind me on the way to Yate and had said
to his companion, 'Do not be in too much of a hurry', I went

[4]Ta'unga (1847a, p. 22) says 'I threw the spears back at them and they
fled'. Turner (1861, p. 417) records these events with some differences of
detail.
[5]Kabwa is the traditional name for the Noumea-Dumbea area.

over and greeted him, for he too was to be killed that day. I went to the chiefs and Dikadu called out, 'What did you come here for? Who came to fetch you? Go on, leave, for it is sacred where you are. Do not tread there or you shall die.'

I answered saying, 'I came to see the dead man. What is everyone doing — looking at the live man?' He replied, 'No. Who told you to come and see our food?' I said, 'Can't I eat? Aren't you going to feed me? Am I not your guest?' and he answered, 'Yes. You are right. Stay.'

They were very happy and the ovens were burning and it was nearly time to kill the second man. Then I called out saying, 'Share out our man. Give me my share for I must go.' And they answered, 'Wait till the other has been killed. When that is done, then they will be divided out.' But I insisted, 'Divide them. Give me my share.' So they brought me one of the arms and I called out, 'I won't accept that. Give me the live man. That is my share — let that be your gift to me.' There was instant silence, not one of them spoke for a long time. At last one called out, 'Let him take the live man', and another said, 'No. He might set him free.' I replied, 'I want him as a servant to cook my food and to weed my food patch', and all the chiefs agreed. Another one called out, 'What happens if he escapes?' I answered, 'I am not taking him so he'll run away. If he runs away, it won't be my fault.' Another one said, 'What is all this talk about? Take him as your servant.' So I got up, untied his hands and feet, and we went off home feeling very pleased. We cared for him well.

Three months later he said he was going to visit his relatives. I said, 'Have sympathy for me, because if you stay away for ever, evil will befall me. You heard what the chiefs said.' He replied, 'I shall be back after just two nights', and he departed.

The following morning the chiefs came to me and asked, 'Did you let your servant go loose?' I replied that he would be coming back. They said, 'He has lied to you. Once he has reached his home why should he return here?' 'Let us wait until tomorrow', I suggested. They said, 'What a waste of good food to set him free'. Next morning he returned with his mother, together with some food. I was overjoyed, and we lived together for a long time.

At the time of Teura's death,[6] that man assisted us to bury him. He lived with us for about two years, right up till the arrival of Mr Murray on the mission ship.[7]   🐟

[6]Teura: see Chapter 4, n. 5.

[7]This man's name was Navie (or Nyavie). He accompanied Ta'unga to Rarotonga in 1846, where he died (Turner 1861, pp. 421, 458).

6

THE EPIDEMICS[1]

⨝When the people realised that a disease had become widespread they would fetch the priests and ask them, 'Where
does this sickness come from?' And the priests would tell
them. It came from another district, that was where it came
from. Some group had fought against them, that was why it
came. And when the people heard, they would make war on
the people of that place.

Many would be killed, brought back and eaten. That was
why wars were so frequent, because of disease. If all the
priests said that a particular priest had caused the disease,
the people would kill him. When they said it was caused by
a particular household, all members of that household would
be killed. Not one would be spared. That was how many of
our mission teachers died and that means were sought to kill
us. Great was our affliction from this very cause, for many
epidemics occurred while we were there and we were blamed
for them. That was why many of us were killed. It was God's
love which saved the rest of us.

The time we were staying on these islands was a time of
serious epidemics. Eight kinds of illness occurred: head illness
(influenza?), dysentery, illness affecting the knees, abdominal
sickness, mumps, sickness affecting the eyes, sickness affecting
the back, extreme weakness of the body.

When the sickness affecting the head began, the high chief
came to our house to ask where the disease had come from.
We told him we did not know. He was very angry. His
daughter was sick with the disease and getting worse. He
told us not to walk about that day but to remain in our
house lest we be overcome by misfortune. Many people were

[1]This chapter is from Ta'unga 1879, pp. 18-24.

sick in all the houses and some of them died. Great was our sorrow on that day. Next morning the chief told us that his daughter was dead.[2]

Then he told us to go and bury the girl. We said, 'Do not bury her yet. Wait until evening.' But he insisted, so we went to his house where all the priests were assembled and we asked the chief who was to bury her. 'You will', he replied. We did so, but when we were returning to our house the chief said, 'Beware! Stay inside your house for ways are being sought to kill you.' We thanked God, for it was He who put this kind thought into the chief's heart. The people of the island had demanded that we be killed but the chief had not agreed. This made the people so angry that they refused him food. Then the epidemic abated, and people stopped dying in their houses.

No sooner had that month finished, when along came another sickness, dysentery, and many people died. This sickness caused the chief to leave his house and come to live with us. He did so in case we were killed surreptitiously. The people would not come near us, for they thought that we were the cause of the sickness. This belief was an obstacle to the work of God.[3] Another reason was that we did not know their language well. We could not converse with them because we had not been on their island very long when all the households were overcome by sickness.

When all the people knew we were living with the chief, a household came to him with four things with which to buy us, so that he would deliver us up to them. But the chief kept those things and on the third night he called all the lesser chiefs and the people of his district to a meeting at his house to tell them about the offer made to him. He spread the articles in front of them but not one man spoke.

After a while the chief called out, 'What is your opinion?' A lesser chief stood up saying, 'Return them. Let us decline their offer.' The chief replied, 'They shall be returned.' So two men went to return those things — the *ngolo, ui, i'i,* and

[2]In a brief account in the 1846a manuscript Ta'unga explained to the chief, 'Well, she had reached her end. That is the way of mankind in this world. Our time is not long. The real land where we stay forever is up above.'

[3]He says (1846b, pp. 56, 58) that at the time of one epidemic almost all the people of the district abandoned the new religion and fled to distant places because of their fear of sickness. Most resumed the worship of idols and only two chiefs, together with their people, remained faithful to the missionaries.

the *mie*. They are the things I wrote about.[4] So we were saved
from death.

While dysentery was still with us, another sickness which
affected the knees overcame us. The legs were completely
bent, making one unable to walk and the patient defecated
on the place where he slept. It was exceedingly painful and
all households were affected by it. The people could not lie
down to sleep. They blamed us saying that we brought all
sorts of diseases to their island, and began to show bad feelings
against us. That was why the inhabitants of a certain district
came to the chief with offers to buy us. When the chief would
not agree they returned in anger saying, 'Leave it until
everyone is dead'. That was why they declared war upon our
district.

It was Sunday when the war began. Everyone from our
village was gathered together to pray when the war party
arrived. The battle started at the end of the village. They
lit fires and burnt all the houses there and, when our people
saw that their village was afire, they ran to engage the
invaders in battle. Fighting continued and six men from the
enemy side were slain, but not one from our side was killed.
Because of this the people regained confidence in us, and
made friendly gestures towards us and gave us food to eat.

This sickness was still prevalent when another affecting the
stomach occurred and a great number of people died. Its toll
continued until the whole island was affected. Then the chief
became ill and we were dismayed in case he died too. We
prayed to God to spare him and He answered our prayers
by letting him live. One district rejoiced in the chief's illness.
If the chief died they were going to kill us. But the chief
recovered and so we were saved.

That sickness was still with us when mumps broke out
again. Then it was followed by a sickness affecting the eyes
and then one affecting the back and the sickness which caused
extreme weakness. The people were so weak that they could
do no work. And all these illnesses reached the Isle of Pines
and the mission teachers were killed and a ship's crew was
massacred[5] because of them.

The reason for the massacre of that ship was that it had
caused a fight and the teachers were blamed because they
sided with the Europeans. When the people got angry with

[4]See pp. 104 ff.
[5]See Chapter 4.

them they escaped to the ship and sailed away. On their return to the Isle of Pines they were all killed. Thus the blame for all the trouble again rested upon us.

We had confidence in ourselves at this period. We had mastered the language of the island and went about preaching without fear. But before long messengers came from the Isle of Pines to the chief where we lived saying that we were to be put to death, not one was to be spared.

We asked our chief why they had come and he told us. The messengers had said that when the teachers on the Isle of Pines were killed, the sickness abated and people died no more.

7

AN ATTACK FROM
THE ISLE OF PINES[1]

⋞The year before 1843 we argued with the people from the
Isle of Pines. They came to us saying, 'The people of the
Isle of Pines have died through you, for you prayed to your
God to kill every one of us. Twenty-one ships have visited
us and they have asked us, "Why do you treat those Samoans
and Rarotongans so well? Why don't you chase them away?
They are the cause of your death. As for us Europeans, we
do not die because we do not have Jehovah".' I said to them,
'Why do you listen to them? They are telling you lies. Of
course the Europeans have the God Jehovah! Wasn't it
Europeans who brought us to you? We are not the cause of
your death. We are human beings like you and we too will
die.' They said 'Whence has death come?' I answered, 'It is
because you have neglected the Word of Jehovah. That is
why you die.' Thus we silenced them.

We asked, 'What is the name of the European who told
you these things?' and they replied, 'Every European'. 'Where
are they from?' and they replied, 'From Botany Bay, China
[Jaina] and Hobart Town [Obadon]'. Many Europeans had
told them the same thing.

Not long afterwards a war broke out between those of
Noumea [Numea] and our side. A chief from Kabwa [Kamba]
was killed in that war. His body was cut up and shared out
to all the people as well as to the chiefs. A portion was
brought to our village and one of the victim's arms was hung
from the ridge-pole of a certain man's house. I went to see
this thing but I ran away aghast. It had been roasted in the

[1]This account is from Ta'unga 1847a with additional material from
the 1879 and 1846b manuscripts interpolated.

oven and the fingernails of the hand stood up like the tentacles of an octopus.

A little later another war broke out when the Isle of Pines came to fight Caledonia. A ship's captain joined in that war. He gathered together all his guns, but when he found out that we were at Tuauru he decided not to come. Thus the war ended. Mr Weleni was that man's name and he came from Hobart Town [Apadaon][2] [1847a, pp. 31-2].

Two months had gone by since the behaviour of the people had changed for the better when we heard that the people of the Isle of Pines were about to come to Tuauru to take us two mission teachers to their island, but the Tuauru people refused to part with us. We teachers would not agree to go either, so there was nothing to do but fight it out.

We were filled with sadness by the news and before long a chief told us, 'It's a trick. They are coming to ask you to go with them but do not agree.' When he left we assembled together to pray from nine o'clock to noon. That was when we finished our service. We were of one mind and that was we were in the hands of God and He would hold us firmly in his power. And when our hearts were quietened we felt more confident and were no longer afraid. It was as if all was peace [1879, p. 27].

The chief of the Isle of Pines soon arrived with all his people in twenty canoes. They came to kill us. When they reached the mainland they slept at Khiri.[3] When they were quite near to our village, Uadota came to us saying, 'Flee to the mountains or you'll die. The chief of the Isle of Pines has come to kill you.' But I said to him, 'We shall not run away to the mountains. Jesus is the highest mountain of all! When He leaves us then will we die.' 'You are a fearless crowd', he said.

We had got all dressed up while we waited for our doom, having placed our souls in the hands of God [1847a, pp. 22-3]. It was in order that our bodies would be clothed before we met with death. We were sitting in our house all dressed up when we heard the children of the village shrieking as they fled through the bush. So we said to ourselves, 'Here they come'. We had just finished our third prayer and were commencing the fourth one when they arrived within sight

---

[2]This may have been Captain Woodin, a sandalwood trader, of Hobart. —D.S.

[3]Possibly Ciri in the neighbourhood of Goro.

9   Isle of Pines canoe
From O'Reilly and Poirier, *Nouvelle-Calédonie*

of our house. We were just finishing that fourth prayer when they arrived outside our house [1879, pp. 27-8].

They formed into lines which reached right to the door. I was sitting in the doorway. Two of them were standing nearby when one mumbled, 'Here's one'. The other said, 'He'll die by and by. When the chief gives the word to kill, kill.' We still relied on the power of God.

One of them called out, 'Here comes the chief'. My heart wept when the chief arrived calling out, 'Ta'unga and Noa. Ta'unga and Noa. Who are you to create all this trouble? Where did you find these things that have caused all our customs and our gods to disappear? Are you chiefs that you should start all these new sayings? And when you are speared later on, who is going to save you then?' [1847a, p. 23]. The chief continued abusing us outside while crowds amassed in front of the doorways and out along the roads. They were armed with their weapons of war: guns, swords and axes.[4] These were shining with grease. The chief had an axe and a spear in his hands while he continued using bad language. We heard the chief's voice calling: 'Ta'unga, Noa and Teura. Your penis. The penis of your fathers. The genitals of your

[4]These weapons were probably either taken from the ships plundered at the Isle of Pines, or earned from selling sandalwood.

mothers. Your own penises will be cut off and they will be
thrown into the fire.'

I said to the other teachers, 'The chief's language is foul',
and they answered, 'We will die'. 'Trust in Jesus', I replied
[1879, p. 28].

I said to my colleagues, 'Let us go forward and welcome
the chief'.[5] But they refused and Noa wept saying, 'Let us die
right here'. So I went alone to meet the chief, walking
between two rows of people until I reached him.

'Greetings', I said when I faced the chief, and he stretched
out his hand to greet me.[6] He placed a hat on my head and
gave me a shirt saying, 'You are saved'. I led him into our
house and each of us greeted him [1847a, p. 23]. All at once
everyone filed into the house, filling it right up. I said to
them, 'Go and stand outside the yam store-house'. They went
out and yams were brought before the crowd. The ovens were
lit, for that was the custom in welcoming visitors. They themselves cooked their own food. When everything had been
eaten, the chief took a manilla hat off the head of one of his
sons and placed it on my head. Then he called to another
son who brought a dark scarf and put it on Noa. Next he
took a coloured shirt and gave it to Teura saying, 'These are
our gifts to you. You are saved. Pray to God for me and my
family, that we may live.' This was similar to their customary
way of behaving towards their own priests. That was the way
they intended it.[7]

I explained to the chief that the real reason we came to
their island was to tell them about the word of Jesus so that
they would be saved if they believed in Him. That was why
we came. He said that his ancestors had not known of Jesus
but that if they had, he would know also. I told him that
their ancestors as well as ours had lived in ignorance and
darkness, not knowing anything about Jesus because the
whole earth was full of sin and God had abandoned them as
a result [1879, pp. 29-30].

I told him about the real God and all the work He had
done and the purity of man when God first created him;

[5]In the 1879 manuscript he adds: 'Let us die in front of the chief.
Don't let us die like rats in this house.'
[6]In the later manuscript (1879, p. 29) Ta'unga elaborates, saying that
when he greeted the chief the chief stepped back and continued to
abuse him. The chief had an axe in one hand and a spear in the other.
When Ta'unga greeted him in the name of Jehovah, however, the chief
stood still, put his axe into his left hand, and shook hands with Ta'unga.
[7]The 1847a manuscript merely states that he gave them food.

his sins later on and the cause of those sins for which the
Devil had been responsible for he had deceived them. Thus
man was doomed to die and from that time onwards all men
sinned. That was why the world was full of idol worship
causing God's anger against man for that sin. Then God's
love grew and He sent Jesus, His only son, so that man would
be saved from those sins. He died and was buried and rose
again on the third night, so that man would be saved from
the Devil [1847a, p. 24].

I explained that Jesus had been raised to the highest by
God, giving Him the most high name of all names, so all
should go down on bended knees to Him; those in heaven,
those on earth, and those below the earth, in the name of
Jesus the Messiah and Saviour. God gave all manner of things
to Him. He was the greatest of all that God created but all
man had to do in order to be saved was to believe and
welcome Him. Those who believed would live, and those who
disbelieved would die. Jesus had chosen us to bring His word
to Matuku and his people so that they may know about Him,
believe and be saved [1879, pp. 30-1].

When Matuku heard these words, he marvelled and said to
me, 'Let us all go to the house where we are staying'. I
accompanied him there and he presented me with a huge
quantity of food which took two men to carry to our house.
'Ta'unga,' he said, 'Would you come to my island?' 'What
about my own chief?' I asked him. 'I am sorry for him.' But
he insisted so I agreed to go. I told my own chief about it
but he refused to let me go. I praised God for delivering us
from Matuku's hands. He was the Devil himself! Who would
dare speak to him but God himself Who speaks to those of
the Devil as well as those who are good! He was the one to
be feared and He was the chief of everyone in this world;
both the good and the evil. That was why I wasn't afraid to
meet Matuku and to speak before him[8] [1847a, pp. 24-5].

In the month of February they returned to their own
island. On the twenty-fourth day of that month, a canoe came
from the Isle of Pines to steal one of us away. When the

[8]Ta'unga later (1879, pp. 31-2) says Matuku told him he had come
to kill them, but was stopped by the power of the teachers' God.
Matuku asked Ta'unga where he got his knowledge and he replied that
God gave it to him. In an earlier manuscript (1848), according to
Pitman, Ta'unga says that Matuku promised to protect him if he went
to the Isle of Pines and that all the people there would renounce
idolatry.

people of our land heard about it they maintained a watch over us and we were not taken. Many times they came to kidnap us during the night, to take us back to the Isle of Pines, but our chief never forsook us. When we came to the month of March, they saw a comet in the sky and they said, 'This is the sign of our death. This is the fire of Jehovah' [1846b, p. 56].[9]   ⇌

[9]William Gill (1856, vol. 1, pp. 207-8) notes that a comet was a recognised omen of disease, war, or death. The heathens, supposing it to be sent by Jehovah, again vowed vengeance on the teachers.

8

SPREADING THE WORD[1]

⪡After the sermon one Sunday, I suggested to my two
friends that we take the word of God to every household
daily. We prayed asking God what He wished us to do, and
when it was over I said, 'We must have courage. The chief
Matuku still hopes to kill us so let us not be killed doing
nothing, rather let us die doing the work of God. Then when
we die it will be good, for the people will know of His Word.'
We did so daily until I was taken away from the island.
Thus everyone heard the word of God.

Some time later I went to another place some distance to
the east. I left on a Monday night. The distance would be
the same as when one travels right round Rarotonga once.
Niwa was the name of that district[2] and Jivamare was the
high chief. I stayed in his house and that night he assembled
his tribe and all his sub-chiefs and we had a discussion. I
asked them if they wanted to hear about the word of God,
and they did, so we held services there and the Word spread
rapidly from that time onwards. Thereafter we went there
regularly on Sundays, not one Sunday was left out.

Soon afterwards I went to the district of Angara [Ungare],[3]
and the chief Rapanini gathered his people but there were
not many of them. There may have been a hundred
altogether. We discussed the chief's intentions and he told
me that his people wanted to adhere to the Word of God.
We began teaching there and the lessons were well received
so we went there frequently. I returned to my village and

[1]From the 1847a manuscript, followed by additional extracts on this
topic from the 1846b and 1879 manuscripts.
[2]Guiart points out that the Niwa were a segment of the Goro people
and that they did not all reside in one place.
[3]The Mont Dore area of the south-west coast.

69

told my friends about my trip and we praised God for having thus assisted us to achieve this success [1847a, pp. 11-12].

When I discovered that the people there had not neglected the Word of God, I henceforth went to Tara some Sundays.[4] The chief gathered all his people together and I preached to them about the great love of Jesus to all the people of the world because they had sinned. God had ordained that man should die for he had sinned and that was why Jesus came so they may be saved and He died to pay for that sin. Those who listen to Him shall live. After our service they raised their voices saying, 'Do not leave us', so I visited them frequently thereafter. Uaoia was the chief there.

Soon after that I went to Vakune. Teuea[5] was the chief there and he was a brother-in-law of the chief with whom I was staying. When I reached his house (it was quite near, about the distance from here to Avarua)[6] he asked me what my trip was about and I said to him, 'Do you wish to receive the Word of God?' 'Yes', he replied. So he gathered his people and I told them about the great love in the world, and that it was because of His compassion that He came. After our service the chief said to me, 'Do not forsake us'. Then I returned to our village, praising God for what He had done, and from that day on we began calling on them regularly.

Not long afterwards I went to Uakutamie, to the district of Tinomumu. He had only twenty people. I told them all about salvation. Then I returned to our village praising the Lord of the work that I was doing.

Some time later a canoe arrived from the Isle of Pines and when it reached us those on board said, 'Matuku requests you all to pray to Jehovah to save him and his people, for death has claimed most of them'. Later again he sent word that we should be killed. The chief's reasoning was understandable. We discussed the matter and prayed to God for Matuku and his island. Soon afterwards I returned to the other side, to Wao [Uao],[7] and I told them about the creation of man and who created the first man and when it was over I came back by road.

---

[4]Guiart says that Ta'unga may be referring either to Tara, the river between Tuauru and Wao, or to the influential Tara clan of Unia.

[5]Guiart suggests that this was probably Te Wea, a chief of Unia, and that Teuvea (p. 40) was possibly the same person.

[6]That is Titikaveka to Avarua, a distance of about ten miles.

[7]South of Yate.

Soon after this the chief of Tiwaka [Suaka] came. Unihini was his name.[8] He came with all his people: a big crowd of them including women and children. They all stayed at our place. He studied our way of doing things and was most impressed by it. I frequently spoke to him in the language of Uea[9] about the ways of God. I had heard that he knew that language, that was why I spoke thus to him. He listened most attentively. They stayed for five nights, for they had come to investigate the Word of God. When his visit was over he went to the Isle of Pines, and when he returned from there he brought me an axe and two articles of clothing saying, 'When your ship arrives, if there are mission teachers on her, give me two of them because I have many people'. A couple of days previously he had come to me secretly saying, 'Wouldn't you come to live on my island?' I said to him, 'What about my chief? He won't agree.' And he replied, 'We'll run away in secret'. 'But', I repeated, 'I am sorry for my chief.' So he acquainted me with his wishes and told me to consider them carefully. He told me the signs by which we would know his island. He told us about a certain islet and said that his island was just past it. After he told me this, he went on his way [1847a, pp. 20-2].

Later the chief of Gradji [Karaji] came to look into the Word of God. He arrived at our house on a Saturday. I asked him, 'Is the Word of God a good thing?' And he replied, 'I don't know'. So I said to him, 'If you really wish to know, you will know'. Then he answered, 'That is why I came, to find out'. So I told him everything about Jehovah the Lord God, who created heaven and earth, the seas, and all things in the heavens, the earth and the seas, even man. I explained how He put the spirit into men. That was the greatest thing of all. And He named all those things that man could eat, choosing him to be ruler of some of the things that He created. Later on man sinned, but God had said, 'He who sins shall die'. And his penalty was death.

It was the Devil who deceived the people, for he was absolutely evil. He was the instigator of all the evils which befell man, namely, the worship of idols, the killing of men, thieving, lying, adultery, vengeance, jealousy, and all evils imaginable and that was why God became angry with mankind for they had all sinned. Thus man was doomed to die,

[8]Guiart identifies him as Unin, chief of the Pwaola clan at Cape Bayes (Poindimié).
[9]Probably Uvea.

but God loved us and sympathised with man's soul which was to end in hell. He sent His son so that man may live and He was born like man himself but later He died and was buried. And He rose again on the third night and thus man was saved from death from then until now. He who believes in Him, his sins shall be cleansed and he shall be saved!

When our discussion was over he asked, 'When the mission ship returns, let there be four teachers for me for my people are very numerous'. Ketuare was his name. On the day of his departure he said, 'Come with me to see my district'. I agreed but my chief he would not let me go. 'You send Noa instead,' he said, 'Don't you go.'

Noa went and was well looked after. He stayed for a month and on his return told us of the goodness of that place and the enormous number of people there. They requested a teacher for themselves so we praised God because He made it possible for us to visit them.

Some time later the son of the chief of the Isle of Pines came to betrothe the daughter of our chief. He stayed at the chief's house. Soon afterwards somebody committed adultery with another of the wives of that young man and trouble began. His two younger brothers came to retaliate, and they intended to take us as payment. It was about that time that Teura died.[10] He died a good death for he intended to reach the side of Jesus. His death was caused by a distended stomach.

When the chief's sons reached our house, it was packed with people. They were all intermingled, our own people and those of the Isle of Pines. Ueiji,[11] who led the attack on Captain Ebrill's ship, was asking me about the various countries in the world. Neither of us knew of the above case of adultery which had occurred that same day.

One of them came and sat behind my back[12] with his axe in his hand. Another seated himself behind Noa, also with an axe in his hand. The one behind my back told the chief, Ueiji, that they were ready to kill us. They were fraught with anger because Ueiji would not allow them to kill us. They

[10]See Chapter 4, n. 5.

[11]Sometimes spelt Uaise in the manuscript, but Guiart gives the correct spelling as Wenyi in the dialects of the Isle of Pines and Tuauru, and Wedji in the dialect of Unia. He was a nephew of the high chief.

[12]This was Buma, one of the high chief's sons (Murray 1863, p. 288).

ran outside and left us. Thus the people of Tuauru discovered their real intentions and a quarrel began.[13]

From the beginning[14] the chief Niuthu[15] was always a staunch believer. He was also named Uadota. He was conscientious and often asked about the ways of God and all He created. He cared for us well and supplied us with food and became expert in prayer.[16]

After him, his younger brother Kumima came regularly to tell me that he wanted to find goodness. I took him aside and taught him the Word of God and how to write and he learnt these things slowly. Not long afterwards he said to me, 'I want to pray'. But I advised him not to be in a hurry. Later he asked again, 'Won't you let me pray?' Then he asked me why I would not agree to his praying, so I said, 'You must relinquish your idols first, then you may pray to Jehovah. He alone can hear you.'

So he brought me his basket of gods, saying, 'Burn them. Now Jehovah will be my God.' He became skilled in prayer. These were his gods, namely, his father's teeth, hair, whiskers, and nails together with some stones and leaves. We buried them. Later a man named Toine brought his gods and we burnt them, burying those which were parts of men.

Later again the chief Kai and his two sons joined us, giving us all their gods.[17] Not long afterwards Kai's younger brother came with all his household and their gods. Then Meune and his family became believers.

[13]According to the account which Ta'unga gave William Gill, these people came with the intention of killing the teachers, and had planned first to arouse an argument over the resurrection of the dead (William Gill 1856, vol. 1, p. 208).

[14]Ta'unga (1846b, p. 59) states more specifically that Niuthu and his people had earlier accepted his teachings but abandoned them during a serious epidemic. They returned to the fold on 28 December 1843.

[15]Guiart identifies him as Neutu of the Newedu clan of Unia. This, he says, is a different person from the man of the same name mentioned on pp. 48, 52.

[16]Ta'unga (1846b, p. 59) adds that he and his people prayed regularly, morning and evening. Niuthu himself preached to the younger members of his household. They all brought their idols to Niuthu and he gave them to Ta'unga. The sorcerers were angry but Niuthu took no notice of them.

[17]An earlier manuscript (1846b, pp. 58-9) says that this occurred on the second night of January 1844. Kai asked Ta'unga to burn his 'gods' but Ta'unga insisted that he do so himself and he did. Kai was the chief with whom Mataio had lived during his illness. Kai's son Keamo was 'courageous in spreading the word of God, telling all the people along the road about it'.

I could see that the Word of God was gradually spreading everywhere. Dame and his son clung firmly to it as did Uaemu,[18] who believed and turned to righteousness. There was Makarue too who died a good convert. Then there were Paulo, Kapia the younger, and Tivaoku who believed. Petani[19] and Jiopa also behaved properly, heeding the Word of God. Uadota the younger and Jea both died in the faith. I often spoke to them about virtuous living and they asked me many times about the Word of God. I told them that He was the Spirit itself [1847a, pp. 25-9].

In the month of May, on the eleventh night, a war broke out and the chief of Noumea was defeated by Tuauru.[20] His right hand was cut off and brought for the chief of our district. But he threw it away saying, 'Let us not eat it. Take it away and bury it.' I was delighted when I heard what he had said. On the twenty-ninth of that month they again went off to battle and six score of men lost their lives.

The reason for the defeat was that a younger brother of the chief of our district prayed to Jehovah above, from a hill, saying, 'Oh, my new God, oh Jehovah, here I am calling to you, with all my people. Give us success in this battle, that we may see evidence of your power. I have heard that there is no other God like you. Please do that for us because we have faith in you.' When he finished his prayer, they fought and the other party was slain.

On his return from the battle he brought his idols and threw them into the fire. His faith in Jehovah increased greatly. Since then he has become a man of prayer. His name is Thoine. Let us pray for that man, that he may become a disciple of Jesus in that huge land. He has a slight knowledge of reading and of writing on slate. He is a man who has great knowledge of the word of God. His prayer showed great understanding. He himself told me of his prayer when they returned from the battle [1846b, pp. 56, 57].

With the coming of the year 1845, the people's behaviour improved.[21] They began to do the right things; they wore

[18]Guiart identifies him as Wamu of Tuauru.
[19]Guiart identifies him as Pedane.
[20]It appears that the Noumea people blamed Tuauru for harbouring the cause of the sickness and attacked accordingly.
[21]William Gill (1856, vol. 1, p. 206) records a letter received from Ta'unga saying 'We have joy: for the word of God is growing in this land of New Caledonia. Many of the people have learnt to read and are attentive to worship every Sabbath-day...'.

suitable clothes; the women kept themselves clad and wore dresses to church. They listened to our preaching and when the service was over they would ask us more about the sermon and we would explain again. A school for the children was started and I took along some Rarotongan books and they were divided with one book to each group of children. Following this the young men came too, suitably dressed in shirts and trousers taken from the two ships which had been plundered at the Isle of Pines. Heathenism was decreasing but the majority of people still wore no clothes. They were still heathens[22] [1879, p. 26].

In the year 1845 the mission ship *John Williams* [Johon Williamus] arrived, and Noa and I went on board.[23] The two missionaries, Mr Murray and Mr Turner, were very concerned about us because of the evil intentions of the people and their continuous threats to kill us. They told us to accompany them on the ship [1847a, p. 33]. 'A ship's captain who called at the Isle of Pines told us that the people of that island intend waging war against your island and that you two will be killed in the month of May.[24] That is why the mission ship has returned early to fetch you' [1879, p. 40]. I asked, 'Where are we going?' They replied, 'To Samoa. We are sorry for you. The captain is also very anxious that you should come.' I said, 'No, I won't go. I am going back ashore.' They replied, 'You will die'. I said, 'I won't die. If I die, I die. If I live, I live.'

Then they both said, 'It is not right that we should just give up our bodies to death. If you persist in going ashore you are sure to die.' I answered, 'Life and death are not matters which are left in my hands'. But they replied, 'Don't be like that. You have not the right to say what is to happen to you. We decide what is right for you. Do not exalt yourself above us.' Because of this I agreed to their suggestion, but when I informed my chief he wept. He and his younger brothers and their wives and children all went ashore weeping. He sent his son and another man to come and get me. When they got aboard I asked them, 'Why have you come?' They replied,

[22]'The people were friendly for a while; helped to build a chapel and a dwelling-house for the teachers...From sixty to seventy gave up working on the Sabbath and attended the services.' (Turner 1861, p. 416).

[23]12 May 1845 (Turner 1861, p. 412). Ta'unga's manuscript gives the year as 1844 but this is an error.

[24]Shineberg suggests that they may have heard the news at Aneityum from Captain Murphy, or from Captain Cheyne of the *Naiad*.

'The chief sent us to get you because he is sorry for you'
[1847a, p. 33]. We wanted to go back ashore to collect our
few belongings but Mr Murray and Mr Turner said, 'Don't go
back ashore or trouble will start. Leave your things.' So we
sailed away to the Island of Mare. Noa returned to Samoa
but I stayed on in Mare [1879, p. 40].   ⇌

Despite the dangers, Ta'unga, with his supreme faith and self-
confidence, did not wish to leave his post, and told Pitman
that 'he had no wish whatever to be removed, but was urged
to do it by the brethren who considered his life was in
danger'.[25] As he was not permitted to return ashore, he was
obliged to abandon his journal 'in which he had carefully
noted down his labours, places visited, desires of the people,
and his narrow escapes from death'.[26]

[25]Pitman to LMS 6.8.1845, SSL.
[26]Ibid. Ta'unga 1880b (which is not reproduced in this book because it
contains no relevant information) suggests that he wrote still further
material about New Caledonia which has not been preserved. He
explained that he could not find some of his writings about New
Caledonia and Mare, and thought he had probably lost them during his
long stay in Samoa. Moreover, under cover of the same manuscript he
sent some additional writings about New Caledonia (not the 1879
manuscript) to Wyatt Gill, and specifically asked him to return them
when he had read them. These, too, have not been traced.

9

THE LOYALTY ISLANDS

On 13 May 1845, the day after leaving Tuauru, the mission barque *John Williams* drew in sight of the island of Mare.[1]

⨳As we approached Mare and Lifu, the missionaries said to me, 'See those two islands over there. Would you prefer to go to Mare or to Lifu?' 'Let me ashore at Mare,' I said, 'and as soon as I hear word from Tuauru then I'll return there. If I see a canoe going there, then I'll accompany it.' I went ashore but I let the two men from Tuauru accompany the captain so that they would see what the rest of the islands were like.

During my stay there I lived in the house of the two Samoan teachers.[2] It was merely a cooking shelter and was in a bad state of repair. Mr Murray and his colleagues asked me to build a proper house, so I built one six fathoms long and we all lived in it. I had very little to do on that island, for even when I had learnt the language the Samoan teachers refused to let me assist in preaching.[3] I remained patient until one day about a month later a son of the chief expressed a wish to become my friend and I reciprocated. He frequently took me to his house where I told him about the Word of God, and His love towards all people. I did this every time I went to his place. And when he learnt those things he abandoned all the customs of his father, and came to live

---

[1]The balance of this account follows Ta'unga's manuscript of 1847a with some additions from that of 1846b.

[2]The Samoan teachers on Mare were Tataio (see p. 24 and note) and a young man Iakopo who had been assistant teacher on Rotuma since 1840 and who had been left on 10 May 1845. Iakopo returned to Samoa in September 1846. — N.G.

[3]For Samoan-Rarotongan rivalry see Chapter 3, n. 27.

77

with me. He became faithful and told everyone what I had
taught him. Many people followed his example.

When the two Samoans found out about it, they said to
themselves, 'His teaching has spread, yet we were here before
him. Now the people follow him. The best thing for us to
do is to go and get that man ourselves. We'll teach him
instead. Let him not be taught by Ta'unga.' But when they
approached him he refused saying, 'If you had taught us from
the beginning, perhaps we would have learnt something. Now
that Ta'unga has come, he has taught us everything and it is
from him that we have learnt all we know. All you have been
doing is eating.' They were greatly shamed and when I
realised that they were jealous because of my work for God,
I asked them about it but they refused to discuss the matter.
From that day on, that chief's son behaved in a Christian
manner. Uanakakame was his name.[4]

The two Samoans ill-treated me and slandered me, but
when the chief heard about it he frequently invited me to
eat at his house. I visited him regularly and he often talked
to me about the customs of his island and all the evil things
he did. He told me that he had plundered Mr Shere's ship
and killed the Europeans on board her. 'There were nine
people on that ship,' he said. 'It had come from Botany Bay.
Another boatload of people from another ship was killed also.
There were seven altogether, including the captain, but the
vessel itself was saved. Yet another ship called here from
Botany Bay and the crew came ashore to trade and see the
sights. But they took our wives. The next morning they again
came ashore and they were slain. There were twelve killed
from that ship but the ship was not damaged. They shot at
us and one of our men was killed.'[5]

I asked him, 'What did you do with the Europeans who
were killed? Did you eat them?' He replied that they were
eaten and that shares were sent to all the clans. One chief
caught a European and took him home alive. He did not
kill him straight away. He lit the oven first, and then placed
a covering on the ground. Next he led the European to the
oven so he could see it. Then he was killed, cooked and
eaten.

[4]Guiart identifies him as Wanakam, the chief of Tawainedre.

[5]Shineberg has identified the three ships mentioned in this paragraph
as the *Sisters, Martha,* and *Brigand* respectively. The numbers of ships
and deaths given by Ta'unga are probably incomplete as they do not
add up to the totals he quotes.

Another boat arrived from a ship which had been wrecked at sea by a water-spout. The survivors reached here on a small boat. A second boat had drifted away but five of those on the boat that reached here were killed. Two others were kept alive. The total number of Europeans who died on that island was as follows: there were nine ships altogether, plus seven men in one boat and five in another, making twelve in two boatloads. Thirty-three Europeans died on that island. Jeiue was the chief's name.[6]

Cannibalism was rife on Mare and their customs were frightening to experience and horrid to behold. The Word of God did not take root there except with Uanakakame who was the only convert. There was a Tongan woman who could read the Bible but her husband was angry with her, and the high chief was very angry with Uanakakame for adhering to the Word of God [1847a, pp. 33-6]. We did our best to please the chief so that he would let the people come to the lessons but he would not agree. We gathered the Tongan man's household together and taught them from parchment charts.[7] We also showed them how to write on slate. The chief was very angry with the Tongan household for listening to the lessons! Why did they take notice of such useless things! [1846b, p. 40].

Jeiue treated us kindly with regard to bodily needs, but he was not partial to the message of God. He would not behave properly on the Sabbath, and the people followed him in his wicked ways, saying evil things to us. He and I quarrelled many times. I tried to persuade him to believe but he flatly refused [1847a, p. 36].

One day, one of the chiefs gave a big feast to which every one of us went. When it was over, it was announced that fighting would resume. We told the chief that he should abandon warfare, but he replied that fighting was a good thing for that was the way they caught their 'fish'. The 'fish' he was really thinking of was human flesh. We said to him, 'Do not do it or you will sin before God'. He went home and spurned our advice.

[6]Guiart identifies him as Yeiw, the chief of Gwahma, and ancestor of the Huaisilin lineage.

[7]There was an even larger Tongan colony at Efate where their headman, Sualo, a Samoan warrior, was connected by marriage with the leading chief. These Tongans and Samoans had been instrumental in bringing teachers to the island.

Later on, he announced that he was travelling to a distant
place and that he would return on the third night. So he
left. On the morning after his departure a war broke out
and seven people were killed. The chief had fled in case we
intervened. On the day of the chief's return he feigned anger
about the war.

About a month later an epidemic of dysentery occurred and
people died one by one in all the districts, even in that chief's
own district. After many people had died the chief asked us the
reason and we told him why the disease came. But he maintained that it was the priesthood of the land who were the
cause; perhaps they were angry with the offerings of food;
maybe with some other thing. Thus they threw the blame for
such misfortunes on to their own idols. They searched and
searched for the reasons for that sickness. One of the priests
was killed, then another two, but still the deaths from the
epidemic increased. So they began shifting the blame for
the disease on to us. We were assumed to be the cause, so
they tried to devise means of killing us. Some time later the
epidemic abated and the people were saved.[8]

In May 1846 another epidemic occurred and it spread from
one end of the island to the other. It began from the head
and developed into a raging illness. If it began in the
morning, by evening the victim was dead, and if it began at
night, by morning the victim was dead. Death quickly
followed from that disease and it was horrifying to hear the
groans of those who were afflicted. Almost everyone was
afflicted. The land was full of weeping and despair for not
one household was free.

When the epidemic was at its peak the chief's household
became affected and all my medicine was used up in treating
them. His family attended worship, but only because they
feared death from the disease.

Shortly after that sickness began, one of the districts sent
a gift to our chief. They said, 'Give us those Samoans that
we may kill them, and the Rarotongan as well'. The chief
took the offering and gathered all his people to discuss it.
One of the men said to him, 'Let us seek some other way of
repaying this gift. Do not allow our friends to be put in their
hands.' So they repaid that offering, but later on another one
was brought. They presented it to the chief saying, 'Give up
those men, that we may kill them'. The matter was debated

[8]Cf. p. 43.

again, and they decided to repay the offering in order that the responsibility for our death would not fall on them.

We remained on Mare but the Word of God did not take root. I visited that chief many times but each time he despised my advice and poured scorn upon it.

A month later the sickness was still raging when a canoe arrived from Lifu. They said that the same disease had spread to Lifu and that the people were dying as a result. They also brought the news that a ship's captain had told the high chief of Lifu, 'It is Jehovah who has killed you. All the islands are consumed by deaths wrought by Jehovah. But in Samoa, and it is really from there that this illness comes, the white men are consumed by death! Likewise when the ships which travel about reach Samoa, the crews dare not go inland for fear of that sickness. No more white men go to Samoa these days. Jehovah is a man-eating god. It is only in the white men's land that nobody dies. That is because the white men have no god. If only you people would live without gods like the Europeans do, you would not die.' It was evil talk which was spread by that ship.

When the high chief of Lifu heard that news he became angry with the teachers and sought means of killing them. He sent a canoe to Mare to inform our high chief, Jeiue, who became angry and embittered. He sent for me and when I went before him, he questioned me as follows:

'Is this news which I have heard really true?' So I asked him, 'What news is that?', and he told me about it and my heart was deeply grieved. I said to the chief, 'Don't you listen to that talk, it is absolutely untrue; it is intended to incite you to anger against us; it is simply a plot. Their words are worthless lies.' And thereafter the chief's attitude towards us mellowed [1846b, pp. 41-3].   ⇜

Early in September 1846 Ta'unga left Mare to accompany the high chief of that island and some of his people on a canoe voyage to the neighbouring island of Lifu, some sixty miles to the north.[9]

⇝Soon afterwards I left for Lifu to witness the growth of the work of God there, for I was most anxious to see whether or not it had made progress. When I reached there I greeted

[9]Gill and Nisbet to LMS 28.10.1846, SSL. This account of his experiences in Lifu comes from the manuscript of 1847a.

Paoo, and Iona and his wife. They were the missionaries who were stationed there to teach the people. They told me about the customs of that island and said that the Word of God had begun to grow there previously but that recently the chiefs and all the people had reverted to their evil ways.[10] They had abandoned righteousness. This was the reason. One of the teachers stationed there had sinned. He had slept with two of the chief's wives. One was Seirauanga and the other was Kokoti; those were the two wives of the chief that he had slept with. Also the two wives of Mataika, he slept with both of them. There was also Naseai with whom he slept. Of the other women he slept with, one was the servant of the chief's wife and the other was a Tongan woman. Three had become pregnant and had given birth to their children and they all named them Zekaria, which was the name of that mission teacher. He was a man from Arorangi, Mr Gill's [Gilo] village.[11] He was a bad example of a man. When he was questioned about his misbehaviour he insisted on concealing it but Paoo persisted in questioning him about it. Zekaria got angry and began beating Paoo. He grabbed an axe to kill Paoo but it was taken from him by two Europeans. Were it not for the Europeans Paoo would have been killed.

Now when I heard that the people had rejected the good way of life I said to Paoo, 'Let us go and see the chief'. So we visited him that night and he called out to us. We sat beside him and I asked if he could converse in the Mare language and he answered, 'Yes'. I said to him, 'Why did you reject the good life?' He replied, 'It was because of that bad incident in which the missionaries were involved. That was why we left. We thought that it was all trickery because Zekaria sinned. They had told us not to steal and not to commit adultery, but he himself committed adultery. That was why we thought they were all lies. So we left.' I said, 'God does not lie. That is His word. But if man has done wrong, God will punish him. He who is faithful unto death shall live. Leave man for he has sinned, but do not leave God because He did not sin. Return and be faithful, then you will receive goodness.' The chief agreed to all this and from

[10]For details of Paoo and Iona see Chapter 2, ns. 36 and 43. The first converts on Lifu were a party of Tongans 'the fathers of whom, a few generations ago, drifted thither in a canoe' (Macfarlane 1873, p. 31).

[11]Zekaria had come to the notice of William Gill when he was stationed at Arorangi, shortly after his arrival in Samoa. For Zekaria's defection see Murray and Turner 1845 and also Chapter 2, n. 43.

then on he faithfully upheld the Word of God [1847a, pp. 37-8].

The chief of Uvea [Uea] and I had a discussion and he had some very good things to say. It was the month of my arrival in Lifu that I went to visit the chief of Lifu and it was there in his house that I met the chief of Uvea. He called me to sit beside him and I did so. He took hold of me with his two hands, seated me facing him and said, 'Where are you from?' I said, 'From Rarotonga'. 'Where is Rarotonga?' he asked, and I replied that I was not quite sure of the location of the island because it was such a long way off. Because the world was round I was not certain where it was. Then he said, 'Is it a day's journey from here to Rarotonga?' I replied, 'It was four months after we left Rarotonga that we reached these islands, because we called at various places, prolonging the journey. If one went direct from here without calling anywhere, perhaps one could get there within two months because it is far away.' He and the chief of Lifu were amazed at this and they laughed. They asked, 'What was your reason for coming to these distant islands? The real reason. Tell us.'

So I spoke to them gently about the good word saying, 'It was because of our sorrow for your being bound up in death. God's love for you was great and He created compassion in our hearts so that we would come and tell you about His love for your souls, so you may know that your souls are of great importance, even though they have been bound up in darkness.'

They asked, 'Do all men have souls? Do we also have souls?', and I replied, 'Not one man is without a soul! Each and every one has a soul.' They said, 'Whence comes the soul?' and I told them, 'The soul comes from God. He created Adam from soil and when He had made him, he looked like a man, from his head to his two feet, but they were useless. And God then breathed life into him, that was his soul, and he became a live man, and that soul was the part that God intended should live. It is only through ignorance that souls die.' 'Have I a soul?' he asked, and I replied, 'Yes, you have a soul'. Then he asked, 'Will my soul die?' and I answered, 'It will die if it does not know salvation'. 'For what reason will it die?' he asked, and I told him, 'It is because of your sins, because you glory in doing evil things. You have been held back by the power of the devil. You are in his hands now and you will not live.' 'How can the spirit be saved?' he asked, and I answered, 'By Jesus who was sent by God. It is in Him that man should believe, and he who believes in Him shall be saved from his own sins and he will be unleashed from the knot in which he has tied himself. It is right that you should believe in Jesus so you will be saved and your own sins shall be cleansed with His blood.' He then suggested that I go with him to Uvea when he returned, so I agreed. But when the people of Mare heard the news a war broke out on that very day and they nearly killed each other because of it. I ran in between them and stopped the two chiefs. So the war stopped, but from then on I would not agree to his suggestion about going to Uvea because it had caused trouble. That chief had a great wish to know the Word of God and he asked that four teachers be sent to him. Uanakei was his name[12] [1847a, pp. 41-3].

One day we went with the high chief of Lifu to a great feast.[13] In the month during which that feast was held, dancing was performed at the home of the man who gave the feast. Now during the period of a feast the people displayed their various skills. This is what they would do. One man would throw a spear and another man dodge it, that was the way they did it. For three days they accumulated the food and other things and all the people gathered, even from distant places. Not one would come empty-handed, each of them would bring some article. Then they would place those things before the chief himself and would swear that they were for him.

This is what they would do next. If the leader lifted his spear, they all lifted their spears in unison; and when he lunged, they all lunged together; and when he dodged, all of them dodged; and when he crouched down, they did so together; and when he stood up straight, all of them stood up straight; and when he held his spear in a certain posture they all did likewise. It was similar to the custom of the Manuao people.[14]

This was how they dealt with the food: each placed his gift on a portion of food. And as each gift was taken, that food would be given in payment for it, and so on until the

[12]Guiart identifies him as Hwenegei, chief of Fayawe in the southern part of Uvea. Hwenegei, incidentally, remained a supporter of the London Missionary Society even when, in later years, most of the island became Roman Catholic.
[13]This account is contained in 1846b, p. 44.
[14]We have been unable to identify who he means by the Manuao people.

gifts were used up. Likewise with the food. When it was all over the people returned to their homes [1846b, pp. 43-4].

The *John Williams* touched at Lifu on the last day of September 1846 and picked up Ta'unga with the intention of taking him back to Tuauru to re-establish the New Caledonia mission. *En route* they sailed for Uvea but were unable to reach the island owing to adverse winds. The ship accordingly put about and bore away for New Caledonia. Before following the course of the subsequent voyage, let us digress a moment on the customs of the islands where Ta'unga had worked until this time.

10

ON THE EATING OF MEN[1]

🙾It is for Pitman [Pitimani], my missionary in Rarotonga, that I have written this account. It is to be taken to him so that he may understand all the customs of the islands where I have been living, that is: New Caledonia, the Isle of Pines, Lifu and Nengone (Mare).

The first subject to be discussed is warfare. They never stop fighting, day and night, month in and month out. The reason they fight so frequently is to satisfy their hunger for human flesh. This is the cause — it is their vindictiveness. Their squabbles are distinguished by their persistence and the ease with which people will engage in a fight. Relatively few people are taken in open warfare. A much greater number are obtained in fighting by stealth, like kidnapping.

When warriors from one place meet a war party from another place, they will not run away. They will not be afraid of death [1846a, p. 1]. Not a single warrior will weaken, not one will flee [1846b, p. 46]. They invariably follow the same pattern; they fight on until one party is defeated. They take no notice of the number of dead; they ignore it until one side is utterly routed. They will not let up. It is the chief they are really after. He is the real goal. But if their own chief is killed their enjoyment comes to an end for it signifies the defeat of that party [1846a, p. 2]. If the chief of one side is taken by the other then the war is over for that period of time [1846b, p. 46]. The defeated become as serfs. They cannot create another chief for themselves, but they will not be attacked again for they have become mere slaves. They will be called by a shameful name, they will be spoken of as slaves, or as 'pigs sewn through the nose with sennit'. I myself

[1]This account is contained in Ta'unga 1846a. Some additional data from his manuscripts of 1846b, 1847a, and 1879 are included.

saw a party of these slaves. They stayed at our place for two whole months. I fed them myself and they cleared our garden, then they moved on to a different household.

Their battles are not over in a single night. Sometimes they go for three or four nights during which time they sleep on the battlefield, but they do not eat [1846a, p. 2]. They are an exceedingly boastful people, and when engaged in warfare they will not rest [1846b, p. 46]. It is their sacred belief that if they eat they will not overcome their enemies, so they only drink water.

Perhaps you will ask, how do they begin their battles? First they unwrap their war gods and, when their incantations to those gods are over, they fight. They take their gods to the battlefield. They do not leave them at home lest they be killed. There is a special god for the eyes — it is to see the spear as it flies towards one. There is a separate god for the ears — it is to detect the hum of the spear and the whiz of the sling-stone. There is another god for the head, lest it be split open. There is a different god for the body lest it be struck with a spear. Yet another god protects the hands to ensure that the enemy does not survive, and there is another god for the feet, that they may be swift in pursuing the foe. There is a different god for their insides so that they will have no fear, and another for their sleep so that they may be aware of attacks by night.

When all their rites have been performed, they fight. As they take the proper ritual precautions, they do not fear the enemy spears. I have seen for myself the true nature of their fighting. Their greatest glory is to be called a warrior and the timid are considered to be useless. They are not well fed [1846a, pp. 2-3].

All the women accompany them to the battle but do not actually take part in the fight. They remain at a distance and when each side meets to fight each party of women stays behind its own side. They take baskets on carrying poles to fetch the slain. Even when one of their own side is killed they rush forward to carry the body away from the battlefield. They scramble for it, cutting it up with a knife called *tuatava*. Then they place the pieces into their baskets, shouting with glee because their wants have been satisfied. And when they see that another has been killed they rush in and grab him. That is how they behave with the dead. The women from the other side do likewise with the dead on their side [1847a, p. 31].

10 Beginning and ending of Ta'unga's letter dated February 1846 to Pitman from Nengone (Mare Island)

Nengone (Mare)   February 9th 1846

To Pitman   to my
          Missionary in Rarotonga
     For him have I written this story,
          to be taken to him, that he might understand
          all the customs of the
          islands I am living in,
          that is, New Caledonia and the Isle
          of Pines, and Lifu, and
          Nengone (Mare).

About warfare
     I am writing
to you Pitman about all the things I
have seen in these islands. This is the first
topic — warfare. They never stop
fighting, in the daytime and at night.

     . . . .

     . . . this story. What is the point of my writing
this account for you. It is so you will
understand the nature of it, then cast it aside.

                    by Ta'unga at Nengone (Mare)

Literal translation of letter opposite

When an enemy is taken, they grab him and chop him up in pieces and give him to the womenfolk who carry him back to their houses [1846a, p. 3]. The thighs particularly are cut up small [1846b, p. 47]. Then they light their earth ovens and cover them up [1846a, p. 3], and when the bodies are cooked they meet together to eat [1846b, p. 47]. The men each take an arm and consecrate it before placing it on the grave of their dead parents. These are then eaten by the priests [1847a, p. 31]. If it is a chief who has been killed they divide his body out to each and every man, woman, and child, so that all may partake of it. They will ask if anyone is without, for not even a child is permitted not to take part lest they all die. All the houses are filled, they just stay at home and eat, and they warm up the left overs in the ovens.

Now I am writing to tell you lest you should want to ask me how they are cooked. This is how it is done. When one household wants to chop its body up, they do so, and when another household wants to cook theirs, then they cook it. They tie the hands together and bundle them up together with the intestines. The legs are bent up and bound with hibiscus bark. When it is completed they lay the body out flat on its back in the earth oven, then when it is baked ready they cut it up and eat it. But in the case of women, only the arms and the legs are chopped off, the body itself is discarded.

Perhaps you will want to ask, 'Is there only one island where they do those things?' I am telling you that it is done in all these islands, not one is different. They are all the same as far as cannibalism goes, except this island of Nengone (or Mare). Here, when a woman dies not the tiniest scrap of her is left, and it is just the same with a man. They are like fish to them. You may say, 'Is it good to look at?' I am writing to tell you that the flesh of man is really dark when it is cooked. You have probably seen the sea-cucumbers on the reef, well, it is just like that. The aroma it gives forth is exactly like that of goat's meat. It does not smell like pork. They despise pork and chicken, but they will not leave off human flesh.

It is not only victims taken in war who are eaten. If one is angry with another, that man will be sought out and killed and then brought in for cooking. It is the same with the younger brother and the elder brother, for when the older brother is angry with his younger brother, and they fight and one of them is killed, his body will be brought in and baked and

ON THE EATING OF MEN 91

eaten. It is the same with the parent and the child [1846a, pp. 3-4], except that in that case only the head will be eaten [1846b, p. 47].

You may ask how they go about the eating. They eat the head first. They crack the skull open and pick out the brains. You will probably want to ask, 'How do you know?' I am telling you that my own eyes have witnessed these things. It is because of what I have seen for myself that compassion grew in my heart for them, for they are so addicted to these evil customs.

This is the reason why they do it so frequently. It is because of vengeance, and quickness to anger, and hunger for human flesh. Their craving for human flesh is irrepressible. When they have that craving they cannot sleep, they simply cannot forget about it. One curious thing is that when a man is alive he has a human appearance, but after he is baked he looks more like a dog, as the lips are shrivelled back and his teeth are bared. Friend, if only you could have seen it! If only your own eyes could have watched! You could never have held your patience. And I go about amongst all these things, distressed because of these horrid customs, and persuading them to abandon them, but they take no notice [1846a, pp. 4-5]. Alas, my friends, if only you could have seen what I have seen you could not possibly have contained yourselves. Their bodies are like the bodies of men, but their habits are of the most horrible type [1846b, p. 48].   ≈

Referring specifically to New Caledonia, Ta'unga tells us that, on the third day after his arrival at Tuauru, a war broke out 'and men were slaughtered in that war'.[2]

≈I followed and watched the battle and saw women taking part in it. They did so in order to carry off the dead. When people were killed, the men tossed the bodies back and the women fetched and carried them. They chopped the bodies up and divided them. Each household got its share, and they were divided between the sub-clans.[3]

When the battle was over, they all returned home together, the women in front and the men behind. The womenfolk carried the flesh on their backs; the coconut-leaf baskets were

[2]The following description is from Ta'unga 1879.
[3]Ta'unga uses the Rarotonga land division *tapere*, but Guiart informs us that he is referring to the patrilineal, patrilocal sub-clans between which the area was divided.

full up and the blood oozed over their backs and trickled down their legs. It was a horrible sight to behold. When they reached their homes the earth ovens were lit at each house and they ate the slain. Great was their delight, for they were eating well that day. This was the nature of the food. The fat was yellow and the flesh was dark. It was difficult to separate the flesh from the fat. It was rather like the flesh of sheep.

I looked particularly at our household's share; the flesh was dark like sea-cucumber,[4] the fat was yellow like beef fat, and it smelt like cooked birds, like pigeon or chicken. The share of the chief was the right hand and the right foot. Part of the chief's portion was brought for me, as for the priest, but I returned it. The people were unable to eat it all; the legs and the arms only were consumed, the body itself was left. That was the way of cannibalism in New Caledonia [Niu Caledonia].

When they hungered for human flesh, they went in groups of a dozen or so into the bush hunting for men and, if unsuccessful, they went in the night to another village and sneaked up beside a house and listened. When the people were fast asleep, they would enter the house and slaughter a man within, and carry him off into the bush. The people within the house of the dead man would wail aloud, and those of another house would call out, 'Don't cry. Tomorrow vengeance will be taken', and the wailing would cease. The next morning war would break out. The reason for man-stealing was that it was a long time since there had been a war and there had been no human flesh to eat.[5]

The captured man would be divided between all the sub-clans, lest some of them should refuse to take part in the coming battle. Then they would fight, and many would be killed, and they would be delighted because plenty of people had been killed, and their appetite would be satisfied.

If the raiding party went through the bush hunting for men, and found one, they would cook him there and eat him, just like a stolen pig, but no portion of the meat would be taken home that day. If a man was stolen in the village they would carry the body inland lest they be caught out.

Women were not killed if they were found in the bush, and nor were women killed in the houses whence men were

[4]He uses the Rarotongan word *rori* which is used for various types of sea-cucumber.

[5]Guiart points out that this confirms Leenhardt's view that cannibalism was largely motivated by the hunger for meat.

taken for killing. If the victim had a wife sleeping at his side, only the husband would be killed, but the woman would be carried off because if one of the raiding party had no wife he would take her as his wife.

If one raiding party met another raiding party in the forest they would fight, and if some were killed they would be cooked there in the forest, and what was left over would be stored on wooden racks, but none of it would be taken home.

I myself saw platforms of human flesh, but I went away and they ate on. I said nothing to them, nor they to me, they simply roared with laughter. When it was all over, fear gripped the land. No one would go alone to any distant place for fear of being caught. People would travel afar only as a war party. They would not just go walking about, and when they travelled they did so in large groups [1879, pp. 2-5]. ⤚

⤙There is something which I forgot to write about previously.[6] I visited Hienghene [Engene] and saw a feast to which all the people came to bring food as tribute to Pasan,[7] the chief who lived there. His son pleaded with him to kill a particular fat man and Pasan agreed. He sent everyone else home but kept the one that his son wanted. The father asked, 'What do you want done? Shall we kill him now?' The son replied, 'Do not kill him. Cut him up alive.' So the chief sent a man to carry out the boy's wishes.

He got hold of the victim and chopped off one of his hands.[8] The man screamed as it was cut off. Then he cut off the other hand, while the victim twisted and squirmed. When that was done he cut off one leg and then the other. But the man did not die. His trunk was the only thing left. Still he did not die. Then the head was cut off and he at last expired. I was overcome with grief and tried to stop them but they would not listen because I did not know their language, so I was unable to tell them of the right way of life.[9]

---

[6]This section is taken from Ta'unga 1847a.

[7]Guiart says that Pasan was a chief of the Bwaxat lineage.

[8]The hands, regarded as the choicest portions, were mainly reserved for the priests.

[9]The Wesleyan missionaries in Fiji had similar experiences. Cutting off the limbs while the victim was still alive was known as *vakatotoga*. The Reverend John Jaggar reported in 1844 a number of such instances,

11   Missionary representation of the son of Pasan asking his father for
the fat man to eat
From the *Missionary Magazine and Chronicle*, no. CL, Nov. 1848

Oh, Pitman! Perhaps you will say, 'Was that the only
occasion on which this took place?' I tell you it happens all
the time. When people come from another district and that
boy begs for one of them, the result is as I wrote above. The
same applies in every district. Now you may say, 'When that
chief dies won't another chief do the same?' It is the standard
custom of their island, handed down from generation to
generation through the chiefly lines. When a man becomes
chief and his first son is born, when the boy grows up as big
as Elizabeth [Elizabeta],[10] he will plead for a human sacrifice
and when he becomes older and has a wife and she bears
him a son then this sacred right of his is broken. He hands
it on to his own son, and when that child grows up, marries
and has a son, that sacred right is inherited by his son. This

including the eating of a captive chief by his relation, Tanoa, chief of
Bau and father of Cakobau.

His hands were tied and he was made to sit before Tanoa, who *kissed*
him while, *with his own hands,* he cut off one of his arms. Having
drunk some of the blood that he had spilled, he then threw the arm
upon the fire to roast, and afterwards ate it *in his presence.*

This and other extracts from the missionary files are reported in Hogg
1958. — N.G.

[10]Probably Pitman's adopted daughter.

has continued from generation to generation, from ancient times until the present day. They told me it was a sacred custom which could not be dispensed with. Any man who interfered with it would die because it was sacred to the chiefs [1847a, pp. 39-41].   ≈

On his return to Rarotonga, Ta'unga recounted to Pitman the following story of a cannibal priestess on Mare, repeated by Pitman in a letter to the London Missionary Society.

≈Her prerogative is to have the hands of all who are slain in war, which she alone, with a few sacred friends, is permitted to eat. Ta'unga waited upon her and with horror saw all the skulls of those she had devoured about her dwelling. He asked who had eaten all these. She replied that she had. When he expressed his wonder at the sight she replied, 'Oh, there is no food so sweet and savoury as that of human flesh; oh! if you did but taste it! There is nothing equal to it.' The hands of all the white people killed on that island were devoured by this woman because they are sacred to their god Makaza whose priestess she is.[11]   ≈

[11]Pitman to LMS 1.12.1848, SSL.

11

ON THE WORK OF THE GODS[1]

❧I am writing to explain to you the nature of their idols, for you may like to know what they are like and how they obtain them. I tell you, they obtain them for themselves, that is how they get them.

When a father dies, his children pluck out the hair of his head and the whiskers of his face and they treasure those things. Then they plant the body in the ground and leave it there for ten nights. Then they fetch all the priests and dig up the corpse to see whether it is rotten. If it is rotten, they twist the head off. They pull out the fingernails and toenails as well. They use the nails to adorn themselves, they cherish them and care for them well, for they are as gods to them [1846a, pp. 5-6]. The gods of the young boys are the right hands of their fathers — so that they may become competent fighters when they grow to manhood. Even the young girls have gods. They are the fingernails of their mothers, to teach them the plaiting of mats and the weeding of food crops, that they may grow strong and active in their work [1879, p. 13].

When a chief dies, the people of the whole district gather to perform their rites. They take all the things mentioned above and give them to a priest to look after for them. Their dead chief is their most important god, he is the god of war.[2] When they go to battle the priest puts the dead chief's

[1]This chapter is based on Ta'unga 1846a which was addressed to Pitman, with additional material from the 1846b, 1847a, and 1879 manuscripts. Ta'unga says that the material in the 1846a manuscript describes New Caledonia, the Isle of Pines, Lifu, and Mare, but his personal experience in each place was of course restricted to certain areas. For comparative information on religion in New Caledonia see Guiart 1962.

[2]Ta'unga (1846b, p. 49) states that this applied to a chief who had *not* died in battle.

remains into a little basket and carries them on to the battle-field. Then the priest will chant and place the outcome of the war in the hands of their dead chief.[3]

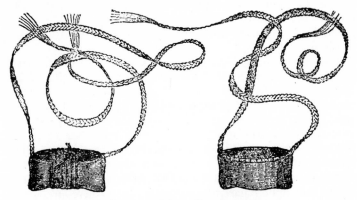

12   Bags containing relics of ancestors
From George Turner, *Samoa a Hundred Years Ago and Long Before*
(London, 1884)

Although they all have gods, the high chief is the greatest of them. Perhaps you will ask, 'Do their gods· have real power?' I tell you that when one man bears a grudge against another he will fetch his own basket of gods and a certain stick and take them to the home of the man against whom he bears malice. There he will hide in the bushes so that he cannot be seen, undo the basket of gods, take out the stick and place it on top of the basket. Then he will mention the name of the man whom he hates, so that these gods will go and strike that man. Then he will return home. Later on that man he hates will die.

You may ask 'Are those all the gods they have?' When one's mother dies they bury her and on the eighth night they dig her up again. They twist off her head and place it in their food gardens and it causes the food plants to grow.[4] The skull itself is placed in their food gardens as it causes the crops to

[3]Turner (1861, p. 427) states that the role of the priests in warfare was to remain at a distance from the fighting, where they would fast and pray for victory. Turner derived his information on New Caledonia from Ta'unga and other Polynesian teachers.

[4]Ta'unga (1879, p. 13) states that the body was buried in a sitting position with the trunk under the ground and the head sticking out. When the head was taken off it was 'put gently into a suitable place in a stream, and when it had rotted further the teeth were plucked out. The teeth were wrapped carefully so they could never decay'.

grow. They treat it as a god, using it to decorate and protect their houses. The fingernails of their mothers are their planting gods.

It is the same when children die. They dig them up again and wrench off their heads, using them as gods to give them strength. They carry them about when they travel from place to place.[5]

They also use a stone, it is a dark stone called *kara* (it is the same as that used to make stone axes in Rarotonga formerly) and they fashion it meticulously until it is perfectly round. They make it quite small so that when it is held in the palm of the hand, and the hand is closed, it cannot be seen. It is about the size of a bullet. It is their god for the heart, so their hearts may be just like stone and never feel afraid [1846a, pp. 6-7].

The eyes have a different god. When preparing it they take the heads of their parents which they use to give strength in fighting. This is the way it is done. They gather certain leaves from the mountains and they place them around the eyes of their parents. Then they place them before their own eyes. Thus the eyes of their parents enable them to see the spears clearly and make them crafty-eyed. It is the same with the ears. They put the leaves of the casuarina tree into the holes of their ears after they have done the same to the ears of their parents. Then they pray to their parents to make their ears hear the rush of spears and sling-stones and do likewise for other parts of the body. Then none of them will be injured for they have come prepared [1847a, p. 31].

When the rain does not fall and all the food plants die because of drought, a priest performs rites to bring rain.[6] He will go to the grave of a dead man and take out all the bones, pack them in a basket, and take them into a cave.[7] The priest

[5]Turner (1861, p. 425), speaking of burial in general, says that at death the body was dressed with a belt and shell armlets, the grave was spread with a mat, and all the body except the head was buried. This applied to both chiefs and commoners. Spears were set up at the head of a chief's grave, a spear-thrower was fastened to his forefinger, and a club was laid on top of the grave.

[6]Ta'unga (1879, p. 14) says that the priests who specialised in this ritual were of the Ngaukhuthu people who lived at Burupwari (sometimes spelt Boulouparis today). These people 'controlled the sun and the rain, the thunder and the hurricanes, the wind and the earthquakes, the sickness, the dew at night, the weakness of the body and the famine'.

[7]Ta'unga (1879, p. 14) says invariably a chief's bones were used and that they were washed clean before the rites were performed. The priest took herbal potions and a gourd of water with him.

will be besmeared with charcoal from the head right down
to the feet.

Inside the cave the priest will join each bone to its counter-
part, fitting each to the next, from the skull down to the foot.
The dark leaves of the giant taro are then laid out on the
floor of the cave and the assemblage of bones dangled above
them. He will sprinkle the water over the bones so that it
spills over on to the leaves. They think that the spirit of the
dead man will carry that water up into the heavens, and turn
it into rain. You may well ask, 'But does it work?' I tell you
that priest will stay there until he dies. On the day on which
the rite is performed he will not eat, neither will he drink.
He just stays there waiting for good fortune in the form of
falling rain. Because of the length of time spent waiting he
may die as he neither eats nor drinks.

Then is it successful? Most certainly it is not. When the
man who does that thing dies, is that the end of it? No, it
is not, for this is a practice to which the family of the man
holds most tenaciously. Perhaps you will ask, 'Is it successful
sometimes?' I am writing to tell you, 'Yes, it is sometimes'.
It is not because of the rites they perform that it is successful,
it is because they do it during the rainy months.

Around February and March some of them do it and they
are lucky because that is the rainy season, that is why their
methods are appropriate then.[8]

It is much the same when there is excessive rain. They take
the bones of a man into a cave and dangle them from the
roof of the cave together with a white stone which they hang
up also. Then they light a fire beneath it and both the bones
and the stone are consumed by the fire.[9] They believe that
the eyes of the dead man are responsible for the rain, that
is why he is baked. It is as though the heavens are dried up
by the dead man as he casts his eyes over the land. And does
it work? Most certainly it does not. Even if the whole cave is
filled with fire and the priest who performs the rite dies, it
still does not work[10] [1846a, pp. 7-9].

[8]Average figures shown by Giovanelli (1953, pp. 55-6) confirm that
this is indeed the height of the rainy season both in Burupwari and Yate
(near Tuauru). In a personal communication McTaggart points out that
the rainy season may be delayed, and at times it does not occur at all.

[9]Probably the white stone was coral rock from the lagoon, as this
disintegrates and changes texture when burnt.

[10]There is a variation in the 1879 manuscript (p. 15) in which he
says that the bones becoming parched was the sign that it would stop

If there is thunder and it becomes too great, those priests are informed and this is what they do. Two stones are stood up together near the entrance of a harbour, and they separate those two stones and pour salt water over one of them. Then they put the rib bone of the chief on the other; and therefore those stones cannot cause any more loud noise. It is because the chief of the thunder stands on one of the stones so that they cannot make explosive sounds.

If there is a hurricane and tremendous winds they carry that chief's remains on to a high mountain and dangle him from a tree facing to windward and his power disperses the hurricane and the winds. When the earth quakes, they take the remains and press them under the white stones to cause the trembling to cease. When sickness occurs they pray to that chief to do away with it. And when the land is overcome by famine, and the crops are exhausted, the people take food to the district of the priests because they think that they are angry.

I myself have been to that place. Many things grow there but they are worthless, giving only the appearance of food. This is because the whole populace brings food for them. That is why they lie. My own eyes have seen their deceitful practices [1879, pp. 15-16].

Once when I went to Kili, I met a man called Kari.[11] I asked him, 'Who is God?' and he replied, 'Tungoe. He is a powerful and mighty god. There's no one to compare with him.' I asked him, 'What did he do?' And he replied, 'He saved us in the war'. So I told him about the real God, Jehovah, the creator of all things, and the guardian of all those things; that He created man, blessed the body and also the soul and that Adam, the first man, had sinned. 'We are descended from him,' I explained, 'and from that time onwards the whole world has sinned and man has been cursed for those sins. That is why the people of the whole world became like you, accustomed to praying to idols, for you say that Tungoe is the God. He didn't create all things; he didn't make the heavens, the earth, the seas and man. He is not the basis of life. You say that Tungoe is made of rock. Ah! but Jehovah created the rock that you idolise. And you, you were also created by Jehovah and he gave you a long life. Also

raining, for what had happened to the bones 'would come to pass to all things in the real world; they would be baked dry by the sun through the spiritual power of that dead chief'.

[11]Guiart points out that the chief of Ouen Island was named Kari.

will he shorten it if he is angry with you. Can Tungoe save you from His hands? Who is there to protect you?' That man became frightened saying, 'I will believe in Jehovah'.

They had two great gods but they just marvelled at them for they did not worship them. These were Tungoe and Tuji. Tuji was in the heavens, he was the shooting star. As for Tungoe, he was a huge rock, and they called it by this name, the meaning being 'a testicle', and when any man came too close to that stone he would get swollen testicles [1847a, pp. 29-30].

Many are the gods they worship. Some are wooden, some are made of stone, some are fish, others are birds. There are various minor gods but their great gods are men [1879, p. 12]. They have no carved idols [1846b, p. 48]. The stone gods are their gods of war and they carry these with them. The name given to one of these gods is Akaeaatu, and another is named Matakite. Yet another is named Akamaara.[12] These three gods are wrapped in leaves and placed in a certain 'war basket', which is hung from the left hand. When they go to the battlefield it is held out in front to divert the spears and stones so that they will not strike.

The dog was a sacred emblem. If they can make a dog go on to the sacred battleground, this is a good omen, indicating that they will win it. Then they start to fight, and their opponents will be defeated.

The warriors also have gods in the form of the teeth of their deceased chief and their deceased parents. They extract the teeth and divide them among the warriors and each of them puts his share into his own 'war basket'. Not one will be left out of the distribution. They are wrapped with the leaves of the paper mulberry and put into the baskets [1879, pp. 12-13]. One basket is hung from the forehead and the other from the arm. The former is to guard the head, for that thing will protect it. The latter does the same for the arm [1847a, p. 30].   ⇐

---

[12]The words he uses have meaning in Rarotongan. It is not clear whether he is adapting the Tuauru word to the nearest sound in Rarotongan or whether he is translating the Tuauru word into its Rarotongan equivalent. The names he gives could be literally translated in Rarotongan as 'Breathe On', 'Beware' or 'Seeing Eye', and 'Remember' respectively. War stones (punyamanya or panyao) of an apparently similar type are described in Leenhardt 1930, pp. 40-1.

12

CUSTOMS MISCELLANEOUS

Matters matrimonial

≷This was their method of obtaining wives.[1] When a girl child was born, some man would go and betrothe her. He would call out to the parents, 'She will be my wife'. That was how it was done, and when the girl grew to maturity, she became a wife for that man. Nobody would object for she was betrothed in childhood; and if any man caused trouble he would be attacked. If the man who betrothed the girl died, and his younger brother survived him, the girl would become a wife of the younger brother. If not, and the man who died had a son, the girl would be reserved for that son. The custom was that when the girl was growing up[2] she would be brought to the house of the prospective husband and would be fed by him until she was fully mature. Then he would sleep with her. In this manner some individuals acquired dozens of wives.[3] If the child was the daughter of a chief, however, the younger brother of that chief would betrothe her as a wife for him. In the case of the daughter of the sister of a chief, the son of her brother[4] would betrothe her for himself.[5] The brother would betrothe the daughter of his sister as a wife for him, or, if not, then as a wife for his son. But if the

[1]Ta'unga 1879, pp. 9-10. This section refers to New Caledonia only.
[2]At about seven or eight years of age (Turner 1861, p. 423).
[3]Turner's version (1861, p. 424), obtained from Ta'unga and Noa, is that while commoners had one or two wives, chiefs might have ten, twenty, or even thirty. As female children were betrothed in infancy to adult men, this could facilitate the acquisition of large numbers of wives by men of high rank and prestige.
[4]I.e. presumably the son of the chief himself.
[5]Guiart states that cross-cousin marriage was generally restricted to certain chiefly lines, and was usually resorted to in order to maintain specific alliances.

second wife and the third wife and so on to the tenth wife all bore children to the one man, and the children grew up to maturity, they would have intercourse with the wives of their father. But the woman who actually gave birth to them was forbidden to them.

If the children had wives, the father was permitted to have intercourse with those wives of his children. It was done this way. If the father wanted the wife of a son, he would say to that son, 'Bring so-and-so to me that I may sleep with her tonight'. The son would agree, then he would go and bring his wife to sleep with his father. It was considered an honour by the children for their father to sleep with their wives, and if the wife of one son was not thus slept with, the son would think evil thoughts like this, 'Why is our father angry with me?' because his father did not sleep with his wife. ☚

Speaking of the Loyalty Islands and New Caledonia as a whole Ta'unga wrote:[6]

☚Their manner of living with women is such that they can take their own classificatory daughters to live with. If, for example, Pa and Iro[7] each had a daughter, one could give his to the other and the other could do likewise. The children are not separated from the parents and the brothers are not separated from the sisters. They are just like pigs or fowls.

If a sister gives birth, she may take her child as a wife for her brother. It is the same with a parent. His child may become a wife for another of his own children. Sons sleep with their father's wives, and fathers may sleep with the wives of their children, if they wish. A man's own children go so far as to sleep with the father's favourite wife. So also does he sleep with the favourite wives of his children. They are quite indifferent.

They do it that way so that their chief will be born from amongst them. If they slept with women from far away, and they bore children, they would never become chiefs. That is the way it is in all these islands, not one is different. It is not clear to whom a particular woman belongs. Not until they live in a particular person's house is it clear whose wife is whose. After a man and a woman have followed their own desires, the man goes his way and the woman goes hers, but when

[6]Ta'unga 1846a, pp. 9-10.
[7]Two chiefs of Rarotonga.

she becomes pregnant, then she returns to the household of
the husband. A man may have many wives. They also steal
the wives of other men.   ⇜

Childbirth[8]

⇜When labour pains began the household was brought
together for the birth. All the people would come to watch.[9]
The woman would lie flat on her back, without any covering
at all and with her legs stretched wide apart. If the child
did not come out at the normal rate, a bamboo stick was
inserted in the external orifice of the mother's vagina in
order to enlarge the opening, to allow the child to emerge
freely. The bamboo was inserted on the under side, down
under the vaginal orifice. The child was born, and when it
fell out it was washed and put on a mat;[10] then it was taken
to the fireside and warmed.[11]   ⇜

Native currency and the selling of men[12]

⇜When a travelling party from some distant place reached
a chief, and the people heard of the visitors' arrival, they took
the four things used in the sale of men. These were the
ngolo, the ui, the i'i, and the mie. This was the nature of
these things.

The ngolo was the fur of the flying fox, plaited up like
sennit, each one hundred long,[13] and when the plaiting was
finished they would tie them together and immerse them in
a potion of herbs made from the roots of the nono[14] mixed
with coral lime. The nono roots were ground up and the furs
soaked in the potion until they became reddish in colour,

[8]Ta'unga 1879, p. 16.

[9]The birth normally took place in the doorway of the house and the
visitors assembled in a circle outside (Turner 1861, p. 423).

[10]Ta'unga uses the term ariki — literally something spread out; it could
be any form of mat or cloth.

[11]Turner (1861, pp. 423-4) quotes Ta'unga and Noa as saying

If it is a boy, there are great shouts and rejoicings. A priest cuts the
umbilicus on a particular stone from Lifu, that the youth may be
stone-hearted in battle. The priest, too, at the moment of the opera-
tion, must have a vessel of water before him, dyed black as ink, that
the boy, when he grows up, may be courageous to go anywhere to
battle on a pitch-dark night...Circumcision is practised 'when the
youth's whiskers reach the hair of his head'.

[12]From Ta'unga 1879, pp. 5-8.

[13]He gives no unit of measure, though he may mean that the skins
were made up in lots of one hundred.

[14]Morinda citrifolia, a small tree.

then they were spread out in the sun to dry. When dry they were ready, as the complete article, and it was called *ngolo*.

The *ui* were made from large spider shells taken from the reef. They were extra big ones on this island. They drilled holes through the middle, and scrubbed them until they were pure white, and inserted their arms through the holes they had drilled. Those ornaments were worn by the men between the shoulder and the elbow. The people of rank used them as decorations when they attended feasts, because those white objects made their black bodies look attractive.

The *i'i* were made from the bones of a large bird, rather like a drake, which lived on the uninhabited islets. Its large leg bone was partially wrapped with the fur of the flying fox which dangled in front of the eyes. The part of the bone which was not covered was inserted in the hair. The covered part was displayed.

A *mie* was a very small object found by the seashore. It was like fine sand with a hole inside. It was very hard. Women and girls gathered them, and threaded them like beads and hung them round their necks.[15]

These things were used in buying men. They were taken to the house where a travelling party was staying. It was done this way.

If the head of the household approved of the purchase, the visitors would be killed and eaten. If he did not approve, he would give those things described above as payment for what they had brought. Then the visiting party would survive. If only one man came and it was intended to kill him, they would not bring a *mie* to buy him. If there were two or three men, only one fathom of *mie* was the price for them. *Mie* was a very valuable thing.[16]

[15]Pitman quotes Ta'unga as describing the *mie* as being 'like a string of very small beads, at the ends of which are fastened two exceedingly beautiful shining things, polished and well rounded' (Pitman to LMS 1.12.1848, SSL). Guiart considers that Ta'unga may have been misinformed about the *mie,* and notes that *mie* was the name of the pearl-shell money which was made by only a few clans; the method of its manufacture was secret. The annular shells Ta'unga describes were, according to Guiart, 'very common on the beaches and could not have been of great value'. Cumpston, on the other hand, suggests that *mie* were probably the hard discs from broken spiral shells. He has observed them on beaches in the area and has heard that they were used as 'money'. Shineberg suggests that *mie* may have been *Cypraea moneta.*

[16]Guiart says, 'The non-acceptance of the presents brought spelt immediate disaster for the newcomers but if the presents were accepted, their

In the event of a battle, if one party was forced to retreat, peace would be restored if they displayed a *mie*. If a man's wife was molested and it was intended to attack the guilty party, but he brought a *mie*, that would save the life of the offender. If something was stolen and the thief was to be killed, but *mie* was brought, his life would be saved, he would not die. If a man ran off into the bush with another man's wife and was not seen again, and it was proposed that his relatives be killed in revenge, their lives would be saved if *mie* was brought as payment. They would not die and the woman would belong to the man who ran off with her because she had been acquired by purchase with the *mie*. It was as though their desire for *mie* was much greater than their feeling for the woman.

If a man wanted to go to meet a relative or friend at a distant place, he would go there on his canoe, and the gift he would take to his relatives would be that same thing, the *mie*.

If a man was cursed, and overcome by sickness, and his household fetched a priest to come and make incantations over him, the household would give *mie* to the priest as payment for his services. If the sick man was made well it was right that *mie* should be given to the priest, but if he did not recover the priest would receive only a short one.[17]

If a man was taken prisoner and his household went to fetch him back from the other side, they would take *mie* and he would be handed over. But if they did not take *mie* he would not be released.[18]

Medicinal[19]

In order to strengthen their bodies and to overcome illness they drink potions made from the various intoxicating plants every morning. This is how they make them palatable. They

---

lives were no longer in danger. Ta'unga has erred, however, in describing the ritual gifts and countergifts at the arrival of a foreigner as buying'.

[17]*Mie* was made in varying lengths and types (Leenhardt 1930, pp. 47-55).

[18]Quoting information given him by Ta'unga, Pitman says that this 'circulating medium' *(mie)* belonged to the chiefs.

With this almost anything can be purchased, and a difference amicably settled, but its chief value is to procure human flesh. For a span's length one man can be procured, for two spans two men, for three spans three men, for four four men. For a little longer length can be purchased a chief... (Pitman to LMS 1.12.1848, SSL).

[19]Ta'unga 1846a, p. 14.

pound up those plants in the sea water, and drink the mixture. It causes them to vomit. They fill their stomachs right up with salt water and the intoxicant. Then they fetch potable water and drink it. The sickness is then defecated out of their stomachs and the feeling of heaviness disappears.

I have tried that remedy and found it good. It lightens the body and the heaviness disappears. I still do it to the present day. I am quite accustomed to it. If they are overcome by illness they do the same thing and feel better. They have used that remedy from ancient times until the present day.   ⪧

The planting of food crops[20]

⪦First of all they ask their deceased parents the question, 'Should I go and plant?' It is because their parents have to approve of it. When they sleep during the night and see in the course of a dream that their parents are all dressed up and their houses are filled with stocks of food, they jump into action. They do the preparatory clearing and when it is done they pluck off the head of their dead mother and bring it to the middle of the garden plot and stand it up there. They pray as follows: 'Stay right here, take care of this food garden, make the garden beautiful and have pity for me in my tiredness, make the crop plentiful so that my fame will spread throughout the land.'[21]

When the prayer is over their hearts will be overjoyed, forever watching the growth of the crop. When it comes to the time of harvesting, they take the very first portion to their chief, to show the love that their mothers had bestowed on them by giving forth the food that they had planted. It was the same with all food crops, both the planting and the presenting of first fruits to the chief. For the yam and the taro, for the sugar cane, the banana and the giant taro. The same custom prevailed when they went fishing. They would seek the help of their deceased parents and when they got a catch they would take a portion to the chief. They acted thus in all months and at all seasons.[22]

[20]Ta'unga 1846a, pp. 13-14.

[21]Ta'unga 1879 (pp. 17-18) adds that this action was to guard against all bad creatures which might eat the food, and that the women also planted the fingernails, teeth, eyelashes, and hair of their dead mothers in the food gardens. 'The head was a guard, the teeth were to speak and tell the crops to grow, the eyes were to watch and the eyebrows to make the crops luxuriant.'

[22]Ta'unga 1879 (p. 17) adds that, if there was a big harvest, after giving

When they planted, they observed a particular custom:
they did not sleep with their wives. Nor did they eat bad
fish which it was not appropriate to eat during that work.
These were the *urua*, the *parangi*, and the *maito*[22] as well as
the turtle and the octopus. They would absolutely avoid these
things lest they die from eating them. Perhaps you will ask,
'Did they follow these prohibitions for long?' I tell you, they
did not. At the time of clearing the prohibition was imposed
and it remained until the crop was seen to be growing. Then
the ban was lifted and they could again consume all those
things which had been forbidden. Then too they could again
sleep with their wives.   ⤕

Ta'unga [1879, p. 18] adds:

⤕Women who were strong at planting were much in demand
by the men. The reason one man had many wives was so
that he could have food a-plenty. If he had many wives, he
would have the same number of food patches. The more
wives he had the more food he could consume and it was a
shameful thing if a man had only one wife. He would not
have much food and he would be teased by the people.   ⤕

About vengeance[24]

⤕These islands have no equal when it comes to vengeance.
Their very natures are truly vindictive. That is why all forms
of evil are widespread here. Vindictiveness is the real cause
of them; that is what causes wars and cannibalism, and fights
between fathers and mothers, elder brothers and younger
brothers, chiefs and their followers, girls and their mothers,
tribe against tribe, chief against chief, the cursing of one by

---

the chief the first portion, they would distribute the whole crop to the
people. 'Food was not simply eaten by the planters themselves. First the
gifts would be given, then afterwards the household could eat.'

[23]Ronald Powell, Fisheries Officer of the Government of the Cook
Islands, has identified these fish as *Scombridae carangidae* (sometimes
known as trevally or kingfish), *Acanthuridae acanthurus* and *Acanthurus
strigosus* respectively. The latter two are sometimes known as surgeonfish
or tang.

[24]At a loss to explain the society in which he found himself Ta'unga
attributed the customs and manners of the New Caledonians not only
to the absence of Grace but to the rampant manifestation of evil.
Vengeance thus becomes a central theme in his historical narrative, a
key to explain all that seemed unnatural and atrocious to him. — N.G.

This is a composite account based on Ta'unga 1846a with additions
from Ta'unga 1879.

another, kidnapping, wife-stealing, raping during the night, and the doing of evil to others. By vindictiveness alone are all these evils caused. You may ask, 'How does it start, and how do they become angry?' I am writing to tell you of its very nature so that you will understand.

If one chief speaks disparagingly to another chief, what was said will never be forgotten. He will go on seeking some means whereby he can get even with the offender. Never, never will it be forgotten until the offender is killed, taken away, and eaten. When the subjects of the deceased chief find out that their leader is dead then a war will break out. Nothing can be done to stop it.

Here is another example. If a parent speaks evil of his own son, the son's heart will become angered against him because of what was said. He will join together with a group of men and plot to kill his own father. When he dies he will be eaten. They do the same thing with their mothers.

When a man's younger brother dies, the reason for his death will be sought, and if it is found that the god of the home of his own mother was responsible for the death, she will be attacked and killed by her own son because of the death of his younger brother. The same would be done for the elder brother.

Likewise with the chief and his followers. If the chief speaks evil against his people they will bear a grudge against him. They themselves may attack and kill him. Sometimes when they are angry they search for something pertaining to the offending chief. If they find his food scraps they will take them before their idols and recite a prayer, telling the idols the chief's name, and the chief will die as a result of it.

If one man steals the wife of another, and is discovered, ways will be sought to get even with him. But if he is not caught they will wait until they see the bones of a fish that man has eaten, or the chewed remains of ti^{25} root, or chewed sugar-cane fibre, or a banana skin. The aggrieved person will pick it up and take it home and place it before his own idols and pray that the offender should die, and he does die [1846a, pp. 10-12].

Alternatively he will take those remains to a sorcerer who will carry them to a sacred place and recite incantations and repeat the offender's name, praying that he should die; that if he goes fishing he will die, that if he goes to fight he will

---

[25]Cordyline.

be killed, that if he eats food it will become stuck in his throat, that if he drinks water he will die, that if he sleeps at night he will die, that if he travels overland he will die; that his children will die; that his home will be acquired by someone else; that his wife will be taken by another; and that his food crops will be stolen. This thing and that thing will all be mentioned by the sorcerer in his prayer [1879, p. 11].[26]

On the other hand, if the prayers are carried out but the victim does not die, the aggrieved person will seek him stealthily by night and if he finds him asleep he will attack and kill him. If the victim is not killed the parents will instruct their children never to forget that injury and when they grow to adulthood they instruct their children likewise. It has been their practice from ancient times until the present day. They will not discard that habit for they are so accustomed to it. It is due to this spirit of vengeance that the Europeans are killed in these islands.

When sickness prevails they try to determine the cause of it. When they experience a disease that they have not known in their former times, they believe that the Europeans must have brought it. Then they attack them. It is because they look for explanations in the way to which they are accustomed. They do not realise that those things are sent by God. That is the nature of their vengeance. Now you will understand [1846a, p. 12].   ⋘

General[27]

⋘Pitman, I am writing to you about the nature of these islands. The nature of their customs is similar in respect of warfare, cannibalism, idols, drought and flood, marriage and the theft of women, the planting of food crops, the bearing of grudges, and the way they seek to strengthen their bodies.

[26]Turner (1861, p. 425) quotes Ta'unga and Noa on the redress which could be taken against a person suspected of having caused deaths by witchcraft:

He is formally condemned. A great festival is held. He is dressed up with a garland of red flowers, arms and legs covered with flowers and shells, and his face and body painted black. He then comes dashing forward, rushes through among them, jumps over the rocks into the sea, and is seen no more.

[27]From Ta'unga 1846a (pp. 15-16) addressed to Pitman. Further general information on the way of life on these islands was given by Noa and Ta'unga to Turner. This is recorded in Turner 1861, pp. 423-9 and 1884, pp. 340-7.

I am writing further to you on several final topics. They are a great people for buying and selling. That is their favourite occupation. They purchase food with certain articles. No single item of a man's property is withheld, they just sell anything. They do likewise with food.

Here is another of their customs. When a man becomes ill and he is close to passing away, then they share out property for the various priests and they pray that the man may live. And if he survives then they will pay out those various articles.

This is a way in which they are peculiar. Some of them just go about naked. New Caledonia and the Isle of Pines are better, they wear loin cloths there and the skirts of the women are quite long. But here on Mare where I am living now, and on Lifu, they simply walk about without even a loin cloth. The women are quite unworthy, they just wander about and are unashamed. They ridicule us saying, 'Why should the body be wrapped up?' They tell us to discard our clothes and just to wander about. They think it good. The women despise us in the same way. But we do not scoff at their going about thus, and they are not ashamed.

Pitman, my friend, this is the end of my letter to you. The customs of these islands are innumerable. I have not written about all of them, lest you should not approve of these matters, and perhaps you may not be interested. Therefore I have omitted the rest of the story. What is the point of my writing this report to you? It is just to let you know about these things. Then cast it aside. 🖙

13

RETURN TO RAROTONGA

Having collected Ta'unga from Lifu the *John Williams*
again set her course for Tuauru, where he was anxious to
resume his labours. Ta'unga was not the only one who was
keen to return, for on board were the two young men of
New Caledonia whom the missionaries had taken away to
Samoa when they picked up Ta'unga.[1] These men had merely
accompanied Ta'unga on board when he had gone out to
meet the mission ship at Tuauru nearly two years earlier.
They had no idea when they did so that both they and
Ta'unga would be persuaded to remain on board and
accompany the ship on its eastward journey.

On 5 October 1846 a ship's boat was lowered at Tuauru
and a landing party rowed for the shore. Ta'unga described
the visit:

As we drew close in to look around we could see that
there were no more people left ashore. The village no longer
existed and all the houses had been burnt down. Not a single
person came to see us. We searched around but there was not
a soul to be seen. We deduced that they had all been slain.[2]

According to William Gill, 'the grass, the bush and even
the lofty cocoa-nut trees, were yet as black as coal . . . Some
distance inland, the smoke of a single fire was seen ascending
which confirmed our opinion that the district was yet in the
hands of the enemy, and that they were lurking in secret in
order to decoy us on shore.'[3]

[1]William Gill and Nisbet to LMS 28.10.1846, SSL.
[2]Ta'unga 1847a, p. 38.
[3]William Gill 1856, vol. 1, p. 210.

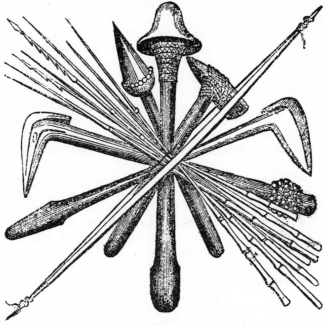

13   New Caledonian weapons
From Turner, *Samoa*

It appears that, 'soon after the removal of the teachers, the people of the Isle of Pines maintained a desperate war with those of the Southern portion of New Caledonia; they slew nearly the whole of the natives who had professed attachment to Christianity, and the warriors were seen by a captain of a whaling ship, who had gone to the island, returning to their homes in all the horrid revelling of heathen victory, with the skulls of the slain stuck on high poles, and their fingers, in almost endless number, hung on strings around the necks of the warriors of the conquering tribe'.[4]

Regretfully they returned aboard. This was the ship's last port of call on this tour of Melanesia and she hoisted sail and drew away for the long slog eastward to Samoa, Rarotonga, and Tahiti. *En route* they sailed through the Loyalty Islands and Ta'unga requested that he be permitted to dis-

[4]Ibid. Gill claims that the reason for the attack was that Matuku had died and his tribe thought that the Tuauru people had prayed for his death. William Gill 1847, p. 60.

embark on the island of Uvea. The two missionaries, however, declined his request.[5]

Beating against the wind it took three whole weeks to reach Niue, the first port of call on the home run. Preparing their report of the mission to the 'heathen' lands while still at sea, the missionaries found that they had a total of twenty-two men then in active service, some with their wives and families. There were nine at Efate, four each at Aneityum, Mare, and Lifu, and one at Niue.[6] From Niue they carried on to Samoa where the ship remained for a month while gifts of coconut oil and other products for the mission were collected and loaded.

Having gone as far as Samoa, Ta'unga decided that he would like to pay a visit to Rarotonga 'to see my missionary, my friends and relations, my son and also the church members and all the people including the students at the mission college. That is the reason for my visit. Then I will return to carry on the work of God.'[7] The *John Williams* bore south from Samoa to Aitutaki, and thence on to Rarotonga, arriving there on 26 December 1846.[8]

Ta'unga was received as a hero, for his work in New Caledonia was well known not only from news conveyed by the missionaries who visited him, but from his own correspondence with Pitman, who read his every letter out in church 'much to the delight of the people'.[9] The day after his arrival home being Sunday, Ta'unga spent the evening addressing the people on his experiences in the islands to the west. The chapel, Pitman tells us, was 'crowded to excess'.[10] Ta'unga was profuse in his thanks to the people of Rarotonga for having prayed for him during his stay in the heathen islands. This, he felt, had been a major factor in his survival against such tremendous odds.[11]

His novelty was no doubt enhanced by the fact that he was accompanied by Navie, the man whose life he had saved after the Yate incident, and who thereupon became Ta'unga's devoted servant. Navie followed Ta'unga everywhere he went

[5]Ta'unga 1847a, p. 38.
[6]William Gill 1847, p. 41.
[7]Ta'unga 1847a, p. 38.
[8]William Gill 1847, p. 63.
[9]Pitman to LMS 6.8.1845, SSL.
[10]Pitman to LMS 27.12.1846, SSL.
[11]Pitman to LMS 26.12.1846, SSL.

in Rarotonga.[12] Ta'unga, too, was delighted to be among his own people again. 'I am very happy indeed to know that Pitman is still alive,' he wrote, 'and the church members, the old people, the young and all the rest of the people. I jump with delight as I meet each one of them. May God be praised for making it possible for us to meet at this time, for you have seen my face and I have also seen yours.'[13]

Ta'unga intended his stay in Rarotonga to be brief, for he was exceedingly anxious to return to his chosen work. He planned to settle for a while on the Isle of Pines, for the chief Matuku was now dead,[14] and being aware of that island's political dominance over much of the mainland he felt that by consolidating there first 'very great difficulties

14 A Tuauru man, probably Navie
From William Gill, *Gems from the Coral Islands*, vol. 1

would be overcome in reference to New Caledonia and the Gospel would soon spread all round'.[15]

The European missionaries on Rarotonga decided that, while Ta'unga was awaiting suitable transport to New Cale-

[12]Pitman, Journal, *passim;* Pitman to LMS 26.12.1846, 5.2.1847. Navie died in Rarotonga a few months later (Turner 1861, pp. 421, 458).
[13]Ta'unga 1847a, p. 39.
[14]O'Reilly 1953a, p. 251.
[15]Pitman to LMS 5.2.1847, SSL.

donia, he should be engaged in preparing some elementary
books and tracts for publication in the Tuauru language.[16] It
was also proposed that he should, at the same time, take
temporary charge of the church at Arorangi. This latter
suggestion, however, was not acted upon owing to objections
by Pitman, and Rupe was sent there instead.[17]

Writing in the language of Tuauru, Ta'unga prepared two
books for use on his return to the field. The first was a
compilation of scripture extracts entitled *Kange vi o Jehova,
vi me ti te mo naevure Duauru,* and the second was an
'elementary book in the New Caledonia language', though
its precise title is not known.[18] A thousand copies of each
were printed at the mission press in Avarua under the supervision of William Gill.[19]

When a schooner on its way to Samoa called at Rarotonga
early in October 1847, Ta'unga embarked in the hope that he
might connect there with a vessel travelling to New
Caledonia.[20]

[16]Minutes of meeting at Avarua 28.12.1846, SSL.
[17]William Gill to LMS, February 1847 and 3.7.1847, SSL.
[18]Ta'unga 1847c and d. So far as is known, no copy of either work
has been preserved. They are described in Gabelentz 1860.
[19]Minutes of meeting at Avarua 9.6.1847, SSL.
[20]Pitman to LMS 28.10.1847, SSL.

14

SAMOA

Ta'unga was well received in Samoa, and was accommodated
at the mission headquarters at Malua. When Bishop Selwyn,
the bishop of New Zealand, arrived there in January 1848
aboard the H.M.S. *Dido,* he sent a letter to Turner, the
missionary in charge at Malua, saying: 'It would be a great
assistance if Ta'unga would accompany us in the ship to
communicate with the New Caledonians. I will take the
greatest care of him and attend to his education till I have
an opportunity of sending him back.'[1]

Although Turner had no objection to the Anglican Church
Missionary Society taking over the work of the London
Missionary Society in parts of Melanesia he was reluctant to
hand over New Caledonia to a bishop who was avowedly
unsympathetic to evangelical doctrine. Besides, he hoped that
one of the Presbyterian communions would take over respon-
sibilities there. His courtesies to the visitor appear not to have
extended beyond a formal cordiality, and he declined Selwyn's
request, saying that he had already decided to send Ta'unga
back to the Isle of Pines or New Caledonia at the first
opportunity, together with a European missionary.[2] The
bishop had little alternative but to concur with Turner's
decision, but pointed out that he considered his mission in
New Zealand was much better situated than Turner's to serve
New Caledonia. 'I feel it is my duty to tell you candidly', he
wrote from the man-of-war, 'that I consider New Caledonia
as my own proper field of missionary duty, from which I
cannot be debarred...'. Duplicating their efforts, Selwyn
thought, was both unnecessary and unwise.[3]

[1]Selwyn to Turner 30.1.1848, SSL.
[2]Turner to Selwyn 3.2.1848, SSL.
[3]Selwyn to Turner 5.2.1848, SSL.

As far back as 1836, the United Secession Synod of Scotland had arranged with the London Missionary Society that if the latter body would 'open up' New Caledonia with native teachers they would provide European missionaries to carry on the work.[4] It was generally accepted by the missions at that time that the role of the 'native brethren' was to make initial contacts, establish peace, learn the language and obtain at least nominal acceptance of Christianity and thus to venture their lives in order to, as Pitman phrased it, 'prepare the way for more efficient labourers from privileged Britain'.[5] With the exception of Ta'unga, almost all the Polynesian teachers who had ventured into the New Caledonia area had either been eaten by cannibals or died of disease. Neither peace nor nominal Christianity was assured, and the United Secession Synod of Old Caledonia seemed to have lost its enthusiasm for bringing the light to its less fortunate namesake.

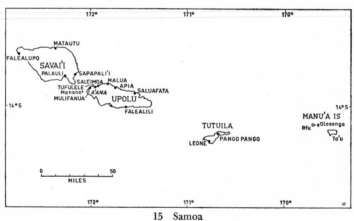

15   Samoa

While the missions continued their negotiations, Ta'unga remained at the theological college at Malua engaged in both teaching and studying, awaiting the day when he could return to New Caledonia. By mid-1849, however, the future role of the London Missionary Society in Melanesia was still not clear, and trouble closer at hand led the Samoan mission to transfer Ta'unga temporarily to Manu'a to take charge of mission activites in that group of islands. The Manu'a chiefs had specifically requested a European, and it was the mission's intention to supply them with one as soon as numbers

[4]Turner to LMS 8.6.1848; Turner to Selwyn 8.2.1848, SSL.
[5]Pitman to LMS 30.6.1847, SSL.

permitted, but they felt that with Ta'unga, assisted by the other teachers already located in the group, 'the wants of Manu'a will be supplied as well as we can do at the present time'.[6]

Ta'unga sailed on the *John Williams* for Manu'a, and was received 'very readily'.[7] He was based at Ta'u, the main village on the island, with a population in 1851 of 820, and from there 'exercised a diligent and well conducted super-intendence over the religious instruction of the whole group'. He operated schools for secular as well as religious education, and was assisted by ten teachers and eleven assistant teachers. The standard of education, particularly at the Ta'u school which Ta'unga personally conducted, was very good by com-parison with other mission schools in the islands at that time.[8] The most promising of the boys were taught in a special class to prepare them for later entry to the theological college on Upolu.[9]

Reports of conditions on Manu'a continued to be encourag-ing, and in 1852 the laws which had been drafted by the mission in Tutuila were adopted on Manu'a and were being observed.[10] The law against tattooing was so rigidly enforced that many young men went to Upolu to be tattooed there.[11] Smoking was not banned by the law, but the mission had established an Anti-Tobacco Association to which all church members and inquirers belonged, as well as 220 children.[12]

Ta'unga's success in collecting contributions was equally gratifying to the parent society. In most of the mission districts in the South Pacific local auxiliary missionary societies were formed in imitation of the parent society. These societies held their annual meetings in May and contributions were collected and sent to the parent society to promote mission work in new areas. Owing to a virtual absence of cash in the early days before settled traders became estab-lished, these were generally made in kind, coconut oil and

[6]Stallworthy to LMS 20.6.1849, SSL.

[7]Murray and Hardie to LMS 15.11.1849, SSL.

[8]Powell to LMS 1.9.1851, SSL. By 1854 more than half the adult population had been taught to read, and 177 children as well (*Samoan Reporter*, December 1854).

[9]Powell to LMS 29.7.1854, SSL.

[10]Murray to LMS 21.1.1852, SSL.

[11]Powell to LMS 3.7.1863, SSL.

[12]*Samoan Reporter*, December 1854. This was seen as an improvement over the situation in 1851 when Powell (to LMS 1.9.1851 and 20.10.1851, SSL) complained of kava-drinking and tobacco-smoking.

arrowroot being the most common items given. From Manu'a in 1852 Ta'unga collected 352 gallons of coconut oil and £3 9s 4d in cash.[13]

During 1854 Ta'unga designed a new church at Manu'a and supervised its construction. According to the mission account it was built of 'stone' but more probably it was coral.[14] When it was completed in the following year, several hundred pigs were slaughtered for the opening feast.[15] Within

16   The old church at Manu'a. It was replaced in 1854 by a church designed by Ta'unga
From Erskine, *Journal of a Cruise*

[13]Sunderland to LMS 26.8.1852, SSL. In 1857 he collected 395 gallons of oil (Powell to LMS 1.1.1858, SSL). The contribution system was a source of endless trouble. Distrust and suspicion were easily aroused when individual sums were not acknowledged in the Society's publications, and those who gave much were disillusioned when little was spent on their own stations.

[14]Powell to LMS 4.7.1855, SSL. The missionaries often referred to coral construction as 'stone'. Coral boulders were bound together with burnt coral lime. This technique of construction, which was introduced by the mission, was widely used in the eastern Pacific.

[15]Powell to LMS 14.1.1856, SSL.

a matter of months, however, it was destroyed by a hurricane, but the people set to with great vigour and rebuilt it during the early months of 1856.[16]

It had not been Ta'unga's wish to go to Manu'a, nor the wish of the Manu'ans that anyone other than a European should be sent to live among them. Although they readily accepted him in the interim, they nevertheless felt a touch of humiliation at being ministered to by Rarotongans, whom they considered a less sophisticated people than themselves. There was no longer any chance of Ta'unga returning to New Caledonia as the London Missionary Society had relinquished its plans for that area. Nor was there much hope of a European missionary, as the number of imported staff was not increasing.

During his first six years on the island the ordinances were administered only when the English missionary from Tutuila came over for that purpose, but in 1855 Ta'unga was appointed to administer them.[17] The people of Manu'a thereupon took the matter into their own hands and stopped taking any collection for Ta'unga's personal support. When Powell, the missionary at Tutuila, asked why, the Samoans simply reaffirmed their request for a European missionary. Powell at length obtained an agreement from the Samoans that they would give Ta'unga one hundred articles annually — anything the contributor wished to give, from a piece of sennit upwards.[18] Three years later, however, there was little improvement, and the directors of the mission in London were informed that the people of Manu'a 'contribute scarcely enough to keep him decently clothed. He feels this unkindness somewhat keenly, but is nevertheless willing to continue at his post.'[19] Ta'unga received no stipend from the mission, only European missionaries being paid a salary. By 1862 the Samoans became resigned to the fact that no European missionary was available (and Ta'unga to the fact of his stay there being relatively permanent) and they commenced making an annual collection of both indigenous and imported products for him, and also permitted him to use their coconut groves to make oil to sell to meet his personal needs for cash.[20]

[16]Powell to LMS 19.7.1856, SSL.
[17]*Samoan Reporter*, January 1857.
[18]Powell to LMS 1.8.1857, SSL.
[19]Powell to LMS 3.7.1860, SSL.
[20]Powell to LMS 3.10.1862, SSL.

Ta'unga maintained himself somewhat aloof from the people of Manu'a, and instead of living in a traditional Samoan *fale* with its thatched roof and open sides he had a large house built for himself. It had coral walls and was partitioned into rooms. Unlike the Samoans, too, he had a modicum of wooden furniture, and even kept crockery and cutlery for the use at least of his visitors.[21]

The role of mediator between European civilisation and the Samoan people fell to Ta'unga as it did to so many of his fellow pastors in the South Pacific in that era. Not only Christianity, but a wide range of culture and custom was introduced through the mission's schools and churches. Ta'unga also acted as physician to the community, dispensing medicines supplied by the mission.[22]

With the pioneer mission field no longer open to him, and with Pitman's warnings about his youthful escapades now well in the past, Ta'unga gave thought to marriage. According to his descendants today, Ta'unga's colleagues in Samoa began pressing him to take a wife, and in fact went to the trouble of pointing out a number of suitable partners. Ta'unga, however, maintained that he should have a Rarotongan wife. At about this time one of the Mangaian missionaries then working in Samoa died of illness, leaving an attractive but forlorn Mangaian widow. The European missionaries saw this as a God-sent opportunity for compromise, for she was of course a Cook Islander like Ta'unga. But he was adamant, a Mangaian would not do.

Ngapoko, Ta'unga's eldest surviving grand-daughter, told us that she had heard the story from her grandfather when she was a little girl. During his visit to Rarotonga in 1847 he had fallen in love with Ngapoko, the daughter of Terei Tamatapu Mataiapo, the holder of the leading chiefly title in the Titikaveka district. At that time Ta'unga felt that his chosen work was among the heathen and that it had not been ordained that he should marry. Once he was settled in Manu'a, however, and he was persuaded to take a wife, he wanted no other than Ngapoko and is said to have sent a message to the Reverend William Gill to arrange to have her sent to Samoa by the first available vessel. She arrived during 1853 and they married almost immediately.[23]

[21]Hope 1866a.
[22]Powell to LMS 14.1.1856, SSL.
[23]A mission report the previous year (Murray to LMS 7.4.1852, SSL)

Ngapoko bore two children, first a son whom they named Tamuera (the Rarotongan form of Samuel), and later a daughter named Maria. Both were born in Manu'a.

It was common in the eastern Pacific in those days for pastors and missionaries to act as interpreters and intermediaries between visiting men-of-war and the indigenous people. Thus when the H.M.S. *Brisk* called at Manu'a in July 1866 to settle the prolonged intermittent war that had been going on between Manu'a and Olosenga, the captain called first on Ta'unga and he joined in the deliberations. When the Manu'a people agreed to negotiate for a settlement, they chose Ta'unga and his fellow teachers to go to Olosenga as their envoys. A peaceful settlement was duly reached and the people of Olosenga, who had fled inland when their coastal villages had been destroyed in the war, were able to return and re-establish themselves.[24]

Not long after the visit of the *Brisk* a volcanic disturbance occurred. It is very likely that it would have been associated in the minds of the people with the conflicts in their society, but no evidence is available on this point. The only account of the phenomenon is the following translation of Ta'unga's diary entries by the Reverend Thomas Powell:[25]

Sept. 7 — There was a very severe shock of an earthquake, which terrified the people.

Sept. 13 — The sea was swollen up like a rock between Ta'u and Olosenga, and the waves broke furiously around the spot. The people thought this was caused by fire. At midday mud was sent up as from a spring. It was now certain that a volcano was forming. In the afternoon the ebullitions were much more violent, and continued till next day, at intervals of about an hour and a half.

Sept. 14 — They now became more frequent, coming every hour, and increasing so much in frequency that they occurred every four of five minutes.

Sept. 15 — The frequency of the eruptions was now at the rate of 49 in an hour up till noon, after which time they

---

noted that Ta'unga had 'applied for permission to visit Rarotonga... with a view of forming a matrimonial connection'. It seems he was not in fact able to undertake the trip.

[24]Hope 1866a and b. Peace did not, however, last for long (see p. 137).

[25]Ta'unga 1892.

came every half minute, the flame flashing through the clouds
of mud, smoke, and stones. The people were much alarmed
by this aspect of things. The sea-water got warm; great
quantities of fish were seen on the surface, of which many
floated to the shore dead, and among them some unknown
monsters and fish of the deep. Men gathered quantities of the
fish, and the land stank with them.

Sept. 16 (Sunday) — Today the eruptions were more violent
than ever, and had increased so much in volume and
frequency that they were now about ten in a minute, and
sent up such quantities of steam and smoke as quite to hide
Olosenga from view; the sea broke fearfully all round the
island; the smoke rose high and dense; masses of dirt were
whitened in the air like floating clouds of slacked lime; all
accompanied by a tremendous noise like air rushing from
below, and in its contention with the sea sending up clouds
of smoke.

Ta'unga says that he now began to think the group would
be rendered uninhabitable; that when the southerly and
easterly winds prevailed Olosenga would be buried, and Ta'u
likewise with northerly and westerly winds.

Sept. 16 to 19 — The frequency and fury of the eruptions
continued night and day at much the same rate as before.

Sept. 20 to 22 — The commotions now increased greatly in
fury and in dimensions; the volcano became like a great
crater, emitting mud and clouds of black, brown, and white
smoke. These discharges of mud and large burning bright
stones and scoriae were sufficient, according to Ta'unga's
conjecture, to fill more than 50,000 men-of-war. Quantities
of scoriae floated on the sea, and were washed ashore along
the opposite coast of Ofu. These discharges were thrown up
higher than the mountain of Olosenga. One volley of rocks
and stones succeeded another so rapidly that the masses
ascending met those descending in mid-air, thereby causing
a hideous concussion and roaring noise. The din was heard
at Tutuila[26] as though close at hand. The eruptions were
seen from there.

Sept. 23 (Sunday) — The violence of the volcanic storm had
now subsided, the eruptions occurring only about once in
every two hours. This much surprised the people, who did
not expect so sudden a change. The clouds of black and
brown smoke were much higher and spread more widely;

[26]Sixty miles from the scene of the eruption.

then they suddenly disappeared altogether, and only the swell of the sea remained.

Sept. 25 — The commotion began anew, with increased frequency and violence.

Ta'unga's estimate of the dimensions of the volcano is this: — It was one hundred feet wide and about half a mile long, or a mile, perhaps, from north to south. It was much nearer to Olosenga than to Ta'u, about two miles from Ta'u.[27]

[27]This paragraph is a note added by Powell.

15

SUCCESS AND TRIBULATION
IN THE MANU'A CHURCH

In 1862, at the request of the Reverend W. Wyatt Gill and for the benefit of his people in Rarotonga, Ta'unga wrote the following report on the arrival of the mission ship and the state of ecclesiastical affairs in Manu'a at that time. In particular he describes in detail the religious revival which had taken place there during the previous twelve months.[1]

⋘On the first Sunday of this month the mission ship arrived here at Manu'a, and on the following morning, which was Monday, the passengers came ashore amongst us. That was on the fifth day of the month. We were delighted to meet the missionaries and the captain and all our friends from Rarotonga.

The missionaries who came on that voyage were Mr Gill [Gili] from Mangaia with his wife and children, Mrs Royle and her children who were going to Sydney, and Mr Pratt [Parati] from Niue with his wife and children. They were going to Savai'i after about five months on Niue.

Mr Powell came too with his wife and children. He is the missionary responsible for our islands. They were to stay here in Manu'a for about five months. Then they were to return to their own island of Tutuila. Some of them returned aboard the ship when the feast ashore was finished. As the missionaries took their places at the feast, the representatives of this island explained their wishes. They wanted a European

[1]Ta'unga 1862. It had not been his wish to come to Manu'a and he lacked the outlets for his talents that the pioneer mission field offered. His scope was limited in Samoa and his writings from there lack the vigour and enthusiasm of his earlier reports.

missionary to themselves. It was difficult to obtain a European missionary but they persisted in their efforts to get one. They were insistent in their request to those European missionaries, and the European missionaries took the request to their meeting.

The people of the island gave seven pigs, fifty green coconuts, forty dry coconuts, and forty taro as presents to the captain and the missionaries. The following morning we took those missionaries who had remained ashore back aboard the ship. The captain had a hard job loading the coconut oil — some of which was for the missionary society and the rest was to pay for the purchase of books. He took 866 gallons aboard.

When we got aboard, we greeted each and every one on the ship, including the wives of the missionaries and all the other women. Meeting them was a great pleasure for us. We gave them encouragement; urged them to be diligent until their very deaths in the work of the Master; to be conscientious in His work; and never to be careless, never to be afraid, never to be apathetic. When it was over, we said our farewells to all the missionaries and all our Rarotongan friends and their wives. The ship sailed on its way and we returned ashore. We thanked God, and praised Him, so that their voyage would be successful, and so God would help the missionaries and the ship's captain, and all the people aboard the vessel; so that He might follow them, right until they landed amongst the heathen; so that no evil would befall them; and so that they would not meet with disaster. If God pleases, we shall all meet again in Samoa with abounding joy. And we praised Him for ever and ever. Amen.

That night we slept at Ofu, and on the following morning we returned to Ta'u. Before he left, Gill told me to write him some notes on what had occurred in this island, right from the early days up until the recent months.

Now I have written the following notes for him:

Mr Gill,

I am writing to you as you requested. Much has happened on this island during the past years that I have forgotten, but I remember the more recent happenings.

Last year (1861) the Word of God spread rapidly, and many of the young people from all these islands sought entry to the church. They continue to do so this year. The work has flourished and some of the seekers have attained full church membership.

In the closing months of 1861 Mr Powell [Paueli] arrived here in Manu'a to inspect our work. I introduced him to the seekers' class and a group of seventeen was admitted to church fellowship.[2] They were voted in by our friends on 16 December.

On 25 January Mr Powell went to Opeta's [Obeda] village, on Olosenga.[3] A group of nine was admitted to church fellowship there. In February another group of twenty-four was admitted, and on the eighth of that month an additional thirteen were accepted. When the work at Opeta's village was completed, Mr Powell came back here to Ta'u. Two of my friends were made deacons for Opeta's village. We were overjoyed because God had caused His work to grow and had given His blessing to these islands.

On the fifteenth day of February a group was admitted here at Ta'u. There were ten of them altogether. And on the twenty-second day of that month a further ten were admitted. On the first day of March 1862 fifteen more were added. Our hearts were gladdened by this compassion shown by God. This was His blessing to these islands. We thought that this was due to the power which had been sent from heaven down to this land. That was why our hearts were full of joy.

We went back to Olosenga with Mr Powell in order to set aside a group for church fellowship. Out of that group, ten were chosen and we brought them here to Ta'u to unite them with our church. We all returned to Ta'u and on 29 March we admitted a further eleven to church fellowship. In the month of April, on the fifth day, we again admitted a further twenty-seven and on the nineteenth of the same month a further group of five. On 3 May another eleven were admitted, and the balance of the population was exhorted to join also.

We set aside a special group from each class of learners, three from Opeta's group, three from mine, and they were sent to the theological college at Malua. They do not go there straight away, first they stay with the missionary in Tutuila. Now all except one who has gone to Malua are at Tutuila with their wives and children. A further ten want to go to college and Opeta and I are teaching them.

[2] The seekers or inquirers consisted mostly of baptised persons preparing themselves for admission into the church on confession of faith.

[3] Opeta was a Mangaian missionary who arrived in Samoa in May 1857. He was appointed to Olosenga and Ofu, and resided at Vaiapi on Olosenga. — N.G.

The seekers' classes are almost finished (as their members have now joined the church) and only a few are left. The majority of them were accepted into the church during recent months: 156 in total.

By the time you arrive at the heathen islands in June or July there will be many more people seeking the salvation of their souls because we have just formed a class for the new seekers. Some people have come to me and expressed their wish to join the work of God amongst the heathen. There are many in my classes now who wish to work for God, perhaps as many as fifty. They are now being instructed and their knowledge is already nearly sufficient.

In the month of August, on the twenty-first day, two men went to Tutuila for further schooling — one from Opeta's class and one from mine. They were accompanied by their wives. Another group is nearly ready to go now, and yet another is nearly ready to go to Malua. Some of them wish to go into service among the heathen.

Our gifts to the mission society are somewhat reduced this year. The gift we have collected is 289 gallons of coconut oil and twenty-six dollars in cash at Olosenga and Ofu, plus 269 gallons of oil here at Ta'u.

Due to good behaviour in these islands we have been blessed by good fortune lately. The chiefs have done their part by sheltering the island, lest evil should grow, and by exercising their laws against this and that. The chiefs are behaving as befits their office, applying the laws that they themselves have made, and encouraging the things which they wish to happen.

They do not countenance any wrong-doing, or anything which is not in accordance with the Word of God. Only that which is right and proper is done by them. That is why the land is so prosperous. And when one of their laws is broken, they seek very carefully to find a punishment which is appropriate to the sin. If the sin is great, the punishment is great. If the sin is small the punishment is small. They are not partial, they do not show favour to the sinner, nor do they consider his standing. They are strong in their insistence on that which is beneficial to the welfare of their island.

The work of the church is progressing well in every way. It is in accordance with the Word of God, and with all the good customs as told us by Jesus. There are still a few who follow heathen customs. They do not behave in accordance with the teachings of the church. They have only the outward forms of piety. The power from above has not entered them. Some of them have slipped backwards. They just follow expediency. The message has not penetrated their hearts, and they soon become weary of doing that which is good.

Those who help in the work of the church are doing very well, and follow the good way of life. They are diligent in giving warning to the people, and they never show favour to the evil-doers. These people do not hold back from telling others of the good work of Jesus, and of the evil which will befall sinners. They are not influenced by the standing of the person concerned. They do not hide the good tidings. They speak their minds openly in the presence of every man.

The children in the classes are behaving well. Some are diligent, but others are dull. There are many who conduct themselves well, only a few do not. The total number of children in my classes at present is 126. There are some of them who have gone to the mission college and others to Tutuila to teach the people there. They have been shared out to the various villages as missionaries. The prospective missionaries are taught in a separate class.

Only the boys and girls go to the school now, not the adults. The youth have combined with the church members and only the young children are left at school. There is nevertheless an early morning class for adults. This class is progressing well and their knowledge is increasing these days. All of them can read, there is not one amongst them who cannot. There are 181 people in the morning class. They can read even big words. They are being taught from the book of Genesis. That is the only reading they are being taught, and the meaning of the words in that book is explained to them.

There is a separate class for the women-folk. There are 120 women in that class. They all know how to read and not one is ignorant. My wife is their teacher. She and I arranged a competition between her class and mine. Her class is of women, mine is of men. But I have been beaten, my wife won the competition! All the women have completed their training and have been received into the church. My group is still struggling along, but hers is finished. She has earned her rest. She only teaches the young girls at present. She has carried out her share of the work faithfully and well.

She has introduced many new customs among the women of the church. They have prayers every single Tuesday, and again on Sunday after the midday service. Those are the times they assemble and pray. It is so that God may bless the Word that is preached to them. They have two prayer meetings on Sundays. When they are over, they all disperse to their homes. Next they teach their children within their households until the drum is beaten for the afternoon service. My wife has also been conscientious in leading the womenfolk in the path of righteousness. The women are delighted with her, and the chiefs also, and so are the children. The missionaries are pleased with her wonderful work, and God is pleased too. She will be a witness of the work she has done in the presence of God. It is as written in Romans xiv 12, 'So then every one of us shall give account of himself to God'. We thank God for His great love to us through His work.

These islands are still pressing for a European missionary to serve them. But the missionaries do not approve of it. Perhaps it will be possible later on. We pray to God that He may bring it about.

Opeta is doing his part at Olosenga and Ofu. His work is progressing; many have been admitted to church fellowship, others have been enrolled in his classes. He and his wife are faithful in doing the work of God. Some of his pupils have qualified for entry to the mission college at Malua, and some are at Tutuila, doing the work of God there. The people appreciate them very much. Their work has been crowned with success. The teaching of the children and of the adults is excellent, as are the other aspects of the work of God. Without doubt it is good.

Likewise the work that Opeta's wife is doing is excellent. The whole village is wearing hats. The women-folk all know how to make hats as she has taught them, and how to sew clothes, and all things relevant to the needs of the body are well provided for. Her teaching of the girls in their village has brought them greater knowledge. But the school is over at present because the people are busily engaged in another work, that is they are building their church. It is nearly finished.

I do not know exactly what the population of their village is at present. Opeta will know about that and he will write it down. It should all be recorded together in one issue of *Te Puna Vai*.[4]

Opeta is administering the ordinances now. He himself carries it out in both Olosenga and Ofu. He is suitable for

[4]*Te Puna Vai Rarotonga* was a mission magazine published in Rarotonga. It was out of print at that time but Ta'unga was probably not aware of the fact.

that work. The people are pleased with him and what he does
meets with success for the love of God is great in these islands.
He has given us bodily health and spiritual blessings. Not one
is left out. God has not sent any sickness to these islands.
The people are all living happily. They are not suffering
from epidemics. Deaths occur but seldom, they do not occur
frequently. Nor are the people often judged for none of them
are persistent in doing evil. There is certainly some evil but
it is not excessive. There is theft, but only occasionally.
Adultery occurs, but it is not common. Fornication is not
habitual the way it is in Rarotonga. Probably that is why
God has shown His love to these islands. The people conduct
themselves well and follow the good way of life.

They pay their native missionaries. Even the people of their
very own islands who are set aside as missionaries are paid.
If it is a great village, then the pay they give to their
missionary will also be great. If it is a small village, the pay
they give to their missionary will be small. That is a very
good way of doing it.

They have a custom that, if a couple goes to the mission
college, then the church members make a collection of gifts
for them to help them during their stay in the college. If one
of them is sent to the heathen islands, the church members
make a collection for him. This is a good system.

To all my friends in Rarotonga, in all three districts, to
the church of Jesus Christ our Saviour. Greetings to all of
you in the name of God. My heart is gladdened to hear the
good news which has come from you; of your good works
and of the growth of the peace of God amongst you, amongst
you in all three districts — in Avarua, in Arorangi and in
Ngatangiia, Titikaveka and Matavera.[5]

Here we are living in a strange land, but still having our
trust in you, remembering all your goodness and your prayers
to God on our behalf. We will never forget them. Your
affection for us flows like a flood of water. Oh, all our friends
in all five villages, never ignore the work of Jesus amongst
you. Never just sit and neglect the Word of God amongst
the heathen for the work of the Master still remains to be
done. Jesus is moving within His churches. He is seeking for
a band of youth from each church, to act as hands for Him,
to carry out His work. As yet they have not been found.

[5]Ngatangiia, Titikaveka and Matavera are sub-districts of the single
district of Takitumu.

Oh friends, oh sisters, have courage! You young people who are within the churches in Avarua, Arorangi, Ngatangiia, Titikaveka and Matavera, be strong in the work of our Master. He has ascended into the heavens, and the work is left for our hands to do. Never yield in this battle. Never be like the city of Meroz, lest your village should be cursed.[6] There is a village in Rarotonga named Titikaveka which is exactly like Meroz. Not a single man has come from there to help in the work of Jesus. Jesus has lived there in that village of Titikaveka for many years trying to convince the people, month by month, year by year, calling out to them. 'For this is the day in which the Lord hath delivered Sisera into thine hand: is not the Lord gone before thee?'[7] Jesus wants his church to be roused, that His enemies may soon be conquered. Some of the people are preparing for the battle, they wish to side with Christ.

The warriors are coming forward, they come through Manu'a here. They are going to the heathen.[8] When a couple arrive, I say to them, 'My brother or my sister, you have come'. Then they will say, 'Here we are. We are going to do the work of the Master.' And when I ask, 'Which church do you come from?' they say, 'From Arorangi'. And when another couple arrives they say, 'We come from Avarua'. Some say, 'We are from Ngatangiia'. Not in a single instance has anyone said, 'We are from Titikaveka'. It is because I am the one who sees every one of them as they go off on their way to the heathen. I am right on the highway of the mission ship, and this is its first port of call. I know all their names and their various villages of origin.

Oh the church of Titikaveka, the churches of every island will stand up and curse you. Those who know that the battle of Jehovah is on, and do not go and take part: see Judges v. 23.[9] If the youth of your village does not take action, this is my word to you, you young folk: Take courage, that you may become as a hand for Jesus, in the doing of His work. Will my eyes ever see some lad or some girl from amongst you? And will you arrive this coming year?

[6]Judges v. 23.
[7]Judges iv. 14.
[8]The mission ship normally called at Manu'a *en route* from Rarotonga to the heathen isles to the west.
[9]This verse reads: 'Curse ye Meroz, said the angel of the Lord, curse bitterly the inhabitants thereof; because they came not to the help of the Lord, to the help of the Lord against the mighty.'

I am overjoyed by the great efforts of my friends from
Mangaia to carry out the work of God. They never hesitate
to undertake His work. Their church should be pleased, it
can never be spoken of as a 'barren woman'. It keeps bearing
many children who go to help the heathen. 'But blessed are
your eyes, for they see: and your ears, for they hear.'[10] They
shall be blessed by Jesus when He returns. He will say to
them, 'Enter thou into the joy of thy Lord'.[11] All our Aitutaki
friends have done great work in persevering with the work
of the Master, and following the proper way of life, and with
showing love for the heathen and for those engaged in the
work of Jesus in every land. The gifts they have contributed
to our friends who are engaged in the work of Jesus among
the heathen show that their love is like running water. It is
a wonderful thing and will help overcome the poverty of our
friends who are working among the heathen. We are simply
amazed by the generosity and liberal spirit shown by that
church. It is a great help to the execution of the work of God
in the lands of the heathen.

May Jesus pour blessings upon them when He returns. See
Matthew xxv. 20 and 21. The love of Aitutaki is just as great
towards those who are doing the work of Jesus in islands
which have seen the light as it is to those among the heathen.
Jesus will not forget their love.

Dear friends, in the mission college in Avarua, this is what
I have to say to you all. Be strong, every one of you, do not
be indolent, that you may be men of courage — fearless
warriors, but not with the weapons of war. Arouse the
remaining islands, that the kingdom of grace may spread
rapidly throughout this world. Let us do the work of Jesus
while we still have a little life. We who have pioneered this
work are now ageing. Our time is short and our end is
uncertain. It is up to God. Pray to God, all of you, on our
behalf, so that our remaining life may be lengthened and we
may continue the work together.

This is my final comment to all the churches, in Aitutaki,
Atiu, and the other islands thereabouts, Rarotonga and
Mangaia. Make haste and pray to God for the work of Jesus
which is being done in every island, here in Samoa, and
Aneityum, Tana, Eromanga, Efate and all the islands there-
abouts as well as Mare and Lifu. Oh my friends, conditions

[10]Matthew xiii. 16.
[11]Matthew xxv. 21.

in those islands are not yet good. Never omit them from your prayers. You must mention them frequently when you pray.

Mr Gill knows the history of all these islands, even those inhabited by heathens. He will explain it all to you. Then you will understand. Pray, learn, come forward and help us.

To you, all the ministers, Gill, Krause [Kalause] and Royle.[12] We will never be forgotten in your prayers for our work. May the peace of Jesus spread rapidly in this world; and may the enemy be vanquished. To all the deacons in all the churches, hasten to pray humbly for good to come to pass in all that is being done, that the work may be fruitful in all the islands where our missionaries are stationed.

Those of us who are engaged in the work of Jesus are anxious that the Holy Spirit may be poured forth over every one of us, and over every place where any of us live. May Jesus grant that it be given. ⤏

In another letter to Wyatt Gill eight years later, Ta'unga made reference to the tribulations that had beset him during the intervening years.[13]

⤏Here we are in Upolu, my wife and I and the children. This is the reason for our visit, it is to see our eldest child, Samuel. He has now been for two years in the college at Malua, and it is because of our love that we came to visit him. Another reason was to fetch medicine for our island from the doctor. We were successful and it is now in my hands. We arrived in Upolu on 24 July and we have been here for two months. Our return to Manu'a is delayed because of the lack of wind. We came from Manu'a on small boats and we will go back by the same means. The mission ship overtook us and it will sail tomorrow, Thursday. We are living together with the European missionaries and our friends from Rarotonga and Mangaia.

Tuka and his wife are still doing the work of God, and Putangi and his wife are helping them.[14] These islands are

___

[12]The Reverend Ernest Rudolph William Krause (1812-73) was at Rarotonga from 1859 to 1867. He had previously served at Atiu (1842), Tahaa (1843), and Borabora (1851). For Royle see Chapter 2, n. 1. — N.G.

[13]Ta'unga 1870.

[14]Tuka from Mangaia went as a missionary to the western islands in 1854, and in June 1857 had landed with Gordon at Eromanga. Neither Gunson nor ourselves have located any information about Putangi.

still troubled by war. Perhaps the missionaries will tell you about it. All I can say is that perhaps we are now nearer to peace. Upolu and Manono and Savai'i are not yet in peace. All the villages there are bad, every one of them. They have not done evil to the Europeans, but they have exhausted the food crops by their raids.[15]

You ask me about the work of God in Manu'a, and I am writing to tell you that it is just the same as before. It has been bad. For two years it was very bad and then it got better. Perhaps you know that little island in the middle named Olosenga. It fought with the island where I stay. Olosenga was defeated, it was utterly routed, and its people went off to Tutuila for about two years. Then they came back to their own island. From that time until now all has been well. Now all three islands are at peace. The church members are behaving well and the native missionaries also. The work is very good and the behaviour of the people likewise. That high chief Tui Manu'a is still living, but he is very old and weak now [pp. 1-2].[16]

You asked me about Opeta. I tell you, he has fallen. He has left us. He was chased out by Olosenga for his wickedness. He beat his wife and she is now separated from him. Powell [Powele] summoned him to Tutuila and he is staying over there now. His place was taken by a friend from Malua.

I send my warm greetings to Sadaraka, and Katuke and Teariki also, and to their wives and their children.[17] I am very pleased at the help they are giving you. Carry on until the coming of the Lord, as it was said 'Enter thou into the joy of the Lord' [p. 3].[18]

I ask you, what about this talk of the missionary Okotai at Pukapuka?[19] There is a party here from Pukapuka and all

[15]For a fuller description of this period of intermittent warfare in Samoa see Gilson.

[16]The genealogy of the Tui Manu'a as recorded by Powell from Tau a Nu'u is given in Pratt and Fraser 1891.

[17]These were Cook Island pastors at Mangaia. Sadaraka had been appointed to the Tamarua church in 1848. Katuke, from Atiu, had been sent by the auxiliary missionary society there to Mangaia in 1844 and was pastor of the church at Ivirua (see W. Wyatt Gill 1885, pp. 56, 61). Teariki from Ngatangiia, Rarotonga, had gone to reinforce the mission at Mangaia early in 1860. — N.G.

[18]Matthew xxv. 21.

[19]Okotai's previous record had been impeccable. He had graduated from the Institution at Rarotonga in 1841, and served on Atiu until

the missionaries have listened to what they have to say. They think Okotai has committed a great sin. Therefore Mr Murray [Male] told me to ask you why Okotai is left to continue in this work [p. 4]?

The war which Ta'unga reported as settled in 1870 broke out afresh in 1871[20] and continued intermittently into the following year. Ta'unga tried desperately to avoid new outbreaks, but one particular battle in January 1872 left twenty dead and eighteen wounded, and another seven were killed in a battle in April. Ta'unga wrote to Powell about the troubles in Manu'a, telling him that no real settlement was yet in sight. Lamenting the situation he wrote:

My heart weeps and mourns for the many who have died in their sins... their souls are lost because, having died in their sins, they are not pardoned by Jesus... They were well instructed and now they have perished in their sins. I am also greatly discouraged on account of the living; many who have joined the war party were in the church, others were preachers, teachers or helpers, but now they are worse than the others, they have become the pillars of Satan's house. And when I... reflect what their end may be I am greatly disheartened, but when I think of God's powers and His love to sinful men, my heart is quietened within me... I pray that the day may speedily come when His word shall be fulfilled — 'He maketh war to cease unto the end of the earth'.[21]

1845 when he was appointed to the staff of the Institution. He then served in Samoa until 1858 when he was left at Pukapuka to assist the Rarotongan missionary there.

[20]Powell to LMS 26.7.1871, SSJ.

[21]As translated by Powell (report to LMS 13.7.1872, SSR). The original by Ta'unga has not been located.

16

SAMOAN MISCELLANY

Ta'unga's visit to the afterworld

Ta'unga left his mark on Samoa. Today legends about him abound, including one to the effect that he died one night and came to life the following morning. We had known of this legend for some years but it was not until 1965 that we had the opportunity to hear a full account. It was told us by Pastor Fiti Sunia (minister of the Congregational Church at Pango Pango) who comes from the Island of Manu'a where his descent group holds the important orator title Fofo. Pastor Sunia says that stories of Ta'unga in Manu'a today mainly concern his strength of character, his forthrightness, and his tremendous devotion to his job. The following story was told to Pastor Sunia by his father, though whether from his own experience or that of the latter's father he is not sure.

On a particular occasion Ta'unga took the Sunday afternoon service and arranged to hold a special class for children that evening. The children gathered in the early evening while Ta'unga was away in the village. When he came home he walked through to the sleeping room at the back of his house and did not reappear. His wife had been entertaining the children until Ta'unga was ready, but he took so long that she went to see what he was doing. She found him dead on the floor. The Samoan custom was that when a person died all the relatives and friends in the village would come and sit with the body during that evening and sing hymns and keep the family company. Ta'unga's wife was so distressed she did not want anybody else to be with Ta'unga except herself and her own children, so she told the Sunday school children that Ta'unga was unwell and sleeping and that there would be no class that night. She then explained to her own children that their father had died. She told them that they would stay with him that night and tell the public in the morning, because once it was known the whole population would come. So they spent the night grieving, Ta'unga's wife reminding the children to sob quietly in case village people heard them, in which case they would not be left alone any more. In the morning Ta'unga's wife told her son to go and tell one of the elder deacons that Ta'unga had died and prepare everything for burial. Just as the boy was moving out the door Ta'unga sat up.

Ta'unga then told his family and the people of the village that when he came in the previous night he felt extremely heavy and lay down. He felt heavier and heavier, and then felt life ebbing away from him and realised that he was dying. He was of the opinion that this was the will of God and he had no power to resist. When he passed away his soul left his body and moved upwards towards heaven but it had not gone far before it met an angel. The angel asked Ta'unga if he would like to see hell, and he said he would. So the angel took him and opened a door and he peeped in and saw a tremendous mass of people crying, wailing, anguished and suffering tremendously. They were immersed in a vast volume of boiling water. As the water boiled it welled up bubbling and great numbers of people struggled to the top and were carried up while others were submerged as the water steamed and surged in waves. He wanted to have a closer look at hell and see which people were crying out and what he could do for them, but as soon as the angel realised Ta'unga's intention he closed the door.

The angel then asked Ta'unga if he would like to see his children who had died. (Pastor Sunia did not know how many of Ta'unga's children had died but the story as told to him was that some of Ta'unga's children died when quite young.) Ta'unga told the angel that he would like to see his children and the children were then presented to him. They recognised their father and he them but as he stepped forward to embrace them the angel drew a dividing curtain between them and the children. It was not clear whether the children were in heaven or some other locality.

Then the angel asked if Ta'unga would like to see heaven and Ta'unga said he would, so the angel took him to heaven and showed him a vast multitude of people smiling and singing and showing every expression of joy and happiness. Some were flying about on wings. He could not see the actual faces of the people and was peering very close when all of a sudden he perceived two particular people whom he knew. These were the only people he could distinguish in the whole crowd at any stage, and one of them was Tui Manu'a Mamana, the deceased high chief of Manu'a, who in life was reputed to have had great supernatural powers. Ta'unga was trying to make contact with these two people when the angel said that it was enough and that Ta'unga would have to rush back to earth because if he did not the people would discover that he was dead and would take his body away and bury it.

The angel took him back to earth and deposited him on a certain hill close behind the village of Ta'u and the soul rushed back and just got into the body at the time Ta'unga's son was being sent off to fetch the deacons to arrange the burial.

The account illustrates some of the views of the supernatural held by Manu'a people at that period. Pastor Sunia was unable to give any indication of the date on which this incident occurred, and was not aware of any other person in Manu'a who was considered to have undergone an experience of this type.[1]

Recording Samoan history

During the later years, with the help of the Samoan chiefs Tau a Nu'u and Tulifua, Ta'unga wrote the history of the Manu'a group of islands, describing in detail the various tribes, titles, and customs of the group. When the mission ship called to collect Ta'unga to return him to Rarotonga, he had no prior knowledge of its coming and had to pack in haste, leaving the bulk of his possessions behind. On his arrival in Rarotonga he wrote back for the history he had compiled, but to no avail.[2] Recent exhaustive inquiries have failed to locate it and it is assumed to have been lost.[3]

The only traditional material that has been preserved from his work in Samoa concerns Karika, a renowned ancestor who had come to Rarotonga from Manu'a about eight centuries earlier. It is contained in a letter to W. Wyatt Gill in reply to his request for historical information.[4]

[1]For detailed analysis of a Polynesian visionary experience see Gunson 1962.

[2]Terei and Haueti 1916, p. 35.

[3]We have, however, located some material recorded by Thomas Powell from the lips of this same Tau a Nu'u, whom Powell describes as the Recorder, or Keeper of Traditions, for the island of Ta'u. Powell 1890, p. 205.

[4]Ta'unga 1870, pp. 2-3.

≋Friend, you asked me, 'Where is the land of Ivanui?' I am writing to tell you that that island is perhaps in the Marquesas. Perhaps it is where Kainuku comes from. It is from there that he really springs. And Makea Karika that you said came from there — definitely not! This is the origin of Makea Karika, on the island where I live, that is on Manu'a. It is said that Makea Karika came from Manu'a. The Manu'a people say it is 'Ari'a.[5] The place he lived was called Aualuma. And his sacred ground is here too. The Manu'a people call it Malaetele and Tangaroa was his God. The place where his canoe was carved out was at Tafagatafaga, and that was the very place he departed from.

The reason that he went away was that there was a fight between one Karika and another Karika. It was a dispute about the chieftainship. Only a small group of people supported the elder brother; most of them joined the younger brother.[6] For about three years the struggle continued and then the elder brother was overcome. Thus the land went to the younger brother who became the High Chief, that is the Tui Manu'a. A great deal is known about the elder brother, Karika (that is Makea Karika).[7]

Now you ask me, 'Do you know of Rongo, the god who was worshipped by the Mangaians in the olden days?' I am writing to tell you that he was a child of Tangaroa. They say in Manu'a, 'Rongo was a child of Tangaroa, he was a god of Manu'a'. He had two names, Rongo and Turi. They were the children of Tangaroa and they were the gods of Manu'a. And Rongona and Lologa — they were the two sons of Tangaroa. Those two were born of the woman named Sina. Sina bore Rongona, she also bore the other Lelologa [sic]. They were the children that Tangaroa had from Sina. She is spoken of in Rarotonga as Ina. Both these men were chiefs of the rank of ariki. Rongona bore Karika the elder and Lelologa bore Karika the younger. Karika the elder is Makea and Karika the younger is Tui Manu'a.

That is all I know of what you asked me. Perhaps this is also known by the old people of Mangaia. Go and ask them

[5]The 'k' in Rarotongan is replaced in Samoan by the glottal stop '.
[6]Presumably a classificatory rather than a real brother.
[7]By genealogical reckoning, Rarotongan tradition records that Makea Karika arrived in Rarotonga from Manu'a in the thirteenth century A.D. After some years of residence on the island, he and most of his followers sailed away to an island called Ivanui never to return. See Pratt and Fraser 1891.

the truth of that story. The story is also known in Rarotonga
is it not?

Preserving breadfruit

In answer to a query from Wyatt Gill, Ta'unga gave the
following description of the preservation of breadfruit in
Manu'a.[8]

A pit is dug twelve feet deep and four feet square. Then
they sew together plantain leaves to line the pit from top to
bottom. Next they pick the breadfruit on the various lands
and prepare the paste there. When the juice runs, they meet
at one pit and store the paste in it. It is left underground
for three or four years. It does not decay. Chestnuts, breadfruit and plantains will grow on top of it. The number of
breadfruit in such a pit would be one thousand each or two
thousand each. The breadfruit pits of the high chiefs are
much more extensive, some being sixteen feet deep and six
feet square, and holding 400,000 breadfruit.[9]

When there is a shortage of food, the paste will be shared
out and everyone in the land will eat it. But if there is
plenty of food each year, it will not be eaten. Every household
has its own preserved breadfruit.

[8]Ta'unga 1880a. This was written after he had left Manu'a.
[9]This is an overstatement, but perhaps unintentionally so as Ta'unga
was not accustomed to the use of such large figures.

17

THE DECLINING YEARS

Return from Samoa

As far back as 1870 Ta'unga had expressed his wish to return to his homeland. He wrote to W. Wyatt Gill from Malua College in Upolu.[1]

❦Oh Mr Gill, my body is strong in the work of our Master, though not quite up to what it was in my youth and my early manhood. My body is weakening, and my work also; the execution of the work is slipping. It is the power of God that does the work. Goodness is growing in the land, the people are following the proper ways, many of them are members of the church, and others are seeking admission. Some wish to go to study at Malua, and some have already gone there. There remains an old group who have been long engaged in the work of God, they help me in the work still.

I wish to return to my own island of Rarotonga but the missionaries here will not permit me to go. It is just the same as you knew it previously [referring to their refusal to allow him to return to New Caledonia]. I will probably die here in Malua, and be buried here, if that is the will of the Lord.

Long have I been in the work of God. I spent five years with the heathen, two years at Malua helping the missionaries there, and twenty-one years here at Manu'a right up until the present time. In total, the years of my service come to twenty-eight.

Friend, my heart was gladdened because you remembered me by your letter. I will never forget you. Continue to write to me so that I will know everything that is going on over there where you are. Write and explain things to me but do

---

[1]Ta'unga 1870, pp. 3-4.

not rush, for your hand grows dark to me, it does not write clearly.

I am delighted by your messages of greeting and by the two baskets of arrowroot you sent. I praise God for them. Who am I that I should be blessed by the Church of God? Tell the church that I have praised their gift to me.

We are living together with the young man Tuka, in his house. But our parting is near at hand, if God pleases to return me to my island. Tuka has cared for us and fed us well.   ⇍

But eight more years were to pass before Ta'unga was finally relieved. The Samoan District Committee approved his retirement in November 1878, and eulogised him for his life of service, but he had to wait almost a year for a replacement and for transport to his home island.[2] He arrived back in Rarotonga with his wife and children on Sunday, 1 October 1879.[3] His son Tamuera was accompanied by his wife Paiau, who was a Samoan, and the daughter (real or classificatory) of the high chief Tui Manu'a. As they did not have a house of their own they stayed at the home of their relation Tairi.[4]

They were welcomed home with feasting and gift-giving in the traditional style throughout the month following their arrival. Each family connected with them by blood provided a separate feast to receive them anew into that particular kin-group. Even those with more tenuous links wished to reinforce their connection with the celebrated couple. 'During that month', says Terei in describing one such occasion, 'Tekari and her husband prepared a feast. One evening, after the lamps were lit, the two of them came to our house bringing food and presents. It was because Tekari was regarded as a classificatory sister of my father, because her father Iro and my father Ta'unga lived together at Titikaveka. That was why she and her husband brought food and gifts.'[5]

Even on his return home Ta'unga did not retire. He was assigned the pastoral care of 430 people (probably but not definitely in his home district of Matavera) and was paid the standard salary of eighty Chilean dollars (then equivalent to about $20 Aust.) per year.[6]

[2]Minutes of Samoan District Committee, 6-10 Nov. 1878, SSL.
[3]Terei and Haueti 1916, p. 21.   [4]Terei 1909, p. 14.
[5]Ibid., p. 23.
[6]W. Wyatt Gill to LMS July 1881, SSJ.

Mauke

Three years after the return from Samoa Ta'unga again went overseas in the service of the church. He was stationed on the island of Mauke to replace Josepha who had been withdrawn towards the end of 1882 because he was 'excessively lazy and given over to novelties of doctrine'.[7] Gill praised Ta'unga's work on the island and spoke of the church there as 'a little gem'. Just how long he remained is uncertain, but a young pastor named Tiavare was appointed to the island in November 1883, and Ta'unga probably returned shortly thereafter.[8] During his service there he attained a standing with the local community which no predecessor, or successor for that matter, has been able to equal. Ta'unga organised the people in the construction of a wall made of coral rock right round their village. This wall still stands. He is remembered to this day as an outstanding leader and is credited with the performance of two miracles during his stay there.

In the first instance some of Ta'unga's possessions were stolen from the mission house. As punishment, so the local tradition on the island runs today, Ta'unga cursed the island and prayed for a famine to strike it. After a severe drought of six months' duration, he repented and again prayed for rain, which fell accordingly.

The second instance concerned a schooner from Tahiti which called at the island to trade. There was at that time a shortage of wine for communion, so Ta'unga and some of the church members went aboard the vessel and asked the captain if he could spare some wine. The captain, it is said, declined the request, and made insulting remarks to the party from ashore. Ta'unga thereupon left the vessel and called upon God to put a curse on it and destroy it. The schooner proceeded on her way to the neighbouring island of Mangaia, but was overtaken *en route* by a violent storm. The vessel foundered off the coast of Mangaia and all the passengers and crew lost their lives with the exception of a woman from Atiu who was washed ashore, thanks to the assistance of a sea monster with which she had a totemic relationship.

These tales are probably *post mortem* and show that in the peoples' eyes he was possessed of great *mana* and held in awe during his pastorate there.

[7] W. Wyatt Gill to LMS 27.7.1883, SSL.
[8] W. Wyatt Gill to LMS 2.11.1883, SSL.

Translations

On his return from Mauke, Ta'unga returned to Ngati Au, to the place of his birth, and built himself a home there. To his dismay, however, he found that during his prolonged absence some of his lands had been used and taken possession of by others. He approached the high chief Pa and Judge Maoate in an endeavour to regain possession but to no avail.[9] Though ostensibly retired on a small annuity from the mission, he continued an active life. He assisted the local minister, Pa Maretu, in his pastoral work, he took over the Arorangi parish for several months when the pastor there was suspended because of his wife's adultery,[10] and he undertook extensive translations for the mission.

The first complete translation of the Bible had been published by 1851, and revised versions were produced in 1855 and 1872. In the 1880s Wyatt Gill felt the need for a further revision and he and Ta'unga worked jointly on the project for several years. Ta'unga knew but little English,[11] but was 'acknowledged to be the best living authority on the Rarotongan language'.[12] When the task was finally completed and the manuscript sent to England for printing, Gill wrote saying: 'If my work is a success, it is due mainly to the untiring aid of Ta'unga....'[13]

Thereafter he devoted himself to the translation into Rarotongan from Samoan (which language he knew well) of a scripture history some 297 pages in length. This history had earlier been translated from English into Samoan by the Reverend George Turner. The Rarotongan version was finally published at the Mission Press in Mangaia in 1896.

Death

Still today the people of Rarotonga tell of Ta'unga and his wife in their declining years. Both aged and thin and white-haired, they were, as one informant expressed it, 'bent over at the same angle'. Wherever was the one of them, there also was the other, and they walked together the two miles to church each Sunday morning.

[9]Many years later, however, after the establishment of the Land Court, Ta'unga's children were able to recover their father's land. Native Land Court, vol. 1, pp. 231-7 and vol. 7, p. 192.
[10]Hutchen to LMS 6.1.1888, SSL.
[11]Hood 1863, p. 37.
[12]W. Wyatt Gill, quoted in Lovett 1899, vol. 1, p. 358.
[13]Ibid.

In the year 1898 Ngapoko was afflicted with influenza and after a short illness she died on 6 August. According to informants today Ta'unga was then in good health and made all the funeral arrangements himself, sending word to the various branches of the family to come and assist. The old couple had been living near the seashore at Ngati Au, but the day after her death the body was taken to a house inland to be prepared for burial.

Having finalised all the necessary arrangements, Ta'unga called his son Tamuera and told him that there was nothing further to be done. He was overcome with grief, and could stand the pain of it no longer. 'We were together throughout life', he said, 'and we will remain together in the parting.' Tamuera remonstrated with him and asked him to consider those of the family who remained behind. Ta'unga reminded him that even the grandchildren were now mature and that he had already informed them of the disposition of his lands and chattels and told them the genealogies and the family history. There was nothing further to remain for, he said, and he could not stand the agony of separation. He thereupon asked Tamuera to carry him inland, and, leaning his head on his son's shoulder, he too quietly died.[14]

In accordance with the old man's request they prepared a double grave on his own land near the seashore. He had chosen the site himself, a spot where he could 'see the ships that sailed on the ocean'. His wish that they be entombed in a single coffin was conveyed by relatives to Mr Jones and Mr Cullen, who were to perform the burial ceremony. This request was declined but the two coffins were placed side by side in a single grave. It is clearly visible today, and distinguishable from other graves in the family cemetery by the breadth of the concrete slab that covers it.

Ta'unga's forebears had been leaders of men in the pre-contact era of Rarotonga, and he himself had excelled in a difficult period of culture change. His only son, Tamuera

[14]The mission's annual report for 1898 (SSR 1.1.1899) says that both Ta'unga and his wife died on the same day. Hutchen (who wrote the report) was at that time absent from the island, but he quotes Jones's diary to that effect. Jones was of course in Avarua, two hours' walk from Ngatangiia where Ta'unga died. Jones gives influenza as the cause of death for both. *Fugitive Papers*, Sept. 1898, also says they died on the same day, but this was published on a different island and was almost certainly given the information by Hutchen.

Terei, was also an outstanding man. He was a member of the Federal Parliament of the Cook Islands[15] and was perhaps the most voluminous writer the island has yet produced. His historical writings have yet to be collated and his own biography written, but in them lies a wealth of information and lore. He was a jovial soul as well as a scholar, and on one occasion when the Resident Commissioner wished to discuss the past with him, he sent him a note of welcome asking him not to be late, 'for by twelve noon the orange beer will be just right and we will partake of it'.[16] Today several of Ta'unga's descendants are studying at universities in New Zealand, and we confidently expect that some of them will one day emulate their ancestor and play a leading role in the current wave of change that is sweeping the Pacific.

[15]*New Zealand Parliamentary Papers* (A3) 1901, p. 9.
[16]Tamuera Terei to Resident Commissioner 19.6.1916, Native Lands Court.

REFERENCES

The location of manuscripts and other rare material quoted in this list is shown in parentheses at the end of the relevant citation. The nature and extent of Ta'unga's own writings are given in more detail than those of other authors and sources.

Buzacott, Aaron, 1842. Journal of a Voyage, Rarotonga (ML).
—, Journal, 31 Mar.-2 July 1842 (SSJ).
—, and Sunderland, J. P. (eds.), 1866. *Mission Life in the Islands of the Pacific,* London.
Cousins, George, 1894. *The Story of the South Seas,* London.
Cowan, C. T. (Tau Puru Ariki), 1961. Personal communication of 7.4.1961.
Crocombe, Ron and Marjorie, 1961. 'Early Polynesian Authors — the Example of Ta'unga', *Historical Studies, Australia and New Zealand,* vol. 10, no. 37, pp. 92-3.
Ellis, William, 1831. *Polynesian Researches During a Residence of Nearly 8 Years in the Society Islands,* 2 vols., London.
Erskine, J. E., 1853. *Journal of a Cruise among the Islands of the Western Pacific,* London.
Felix, R. P., 1951. 'Essai d'établissement des missionnaires à Yaté', *Etudes Melanesiennes* (n.s.), vol. 5, pp. 5-39.
Fugitive Papers, no. 4, Sept. 1898, Mangaia.
Gabelentz, Hans Conon von der, 1860. 'Die Duauru — Sprache auf Baladea', *Die Melanesischen Sprachen,* Leipzig, pp. 214-35.
Gill, William (ed.), 1847. *No te au enua etene i aere ia e te pai orometua 1846* [About the Heathen Lands Visited by the Mission Ship in 1846], Rarotonga.
—, 1856. *Gems from the Coral Islands,* 2 vols., London.
—, 1880. *Selections from the Autobiography of the Rev. William Gill,* London.
Gill, W. Wyatt, 1885. *Jottings from the Pacific,* London.
Gilson, R. P., undated. Samoa: the Politics of a Multi-cultural Community (being prepared for publication), Canberra.
Giovanelli, M., 1953. *Le climat de la Nouvelle Calédonie,* Noumea.
Glaumont, M., 1887. 'Ethnogénie des insulaires de Kunie', *Revue d'ethnographie,* vol. 6, pp. 336-42.

149

Guiart, Jean, 1953. 'Liste par district des villages indigènes de la Nouvelle Calédonie et Dépendences', *Journal de la Société des Océanistes,* vol. 9, pp. 87-90.

—, 1962. *Les religions de l'Océanie,* Paris.

—, 1963. *Structure de la Chefferie en Melanésie du Sud,* Paris.

Gunson, W. Niel, 1959. 'Evangelical Missionaries in the South Seas 1797-1860', Ph.D. thesis, Canberra.

—, 1962. 'An Account of the Mamaia or Visionary Heresy of Tahiti 1826-1841', *Journal of the Polynesian Society,* vol. 71, pp. 209-53.

Heath, Thomas, 1840. Journal 20 Apr.-9 June 1840 (SSJ).

Hogg, Garry, 1958. *Cannibalism and Human Sacrifice,* London.

Hood, T. H., 1863. *Notes of a Cruise in H.M.S. Fawn in the Western Pacific in the Year 1862,* Edinburgh.

Hope, Charles W., 1866a. Journal, London (RPG).

—, 1866b. Report to the Admiralty, vol. 5969, London (PRO).

Hutton, James, 1874. *Missionary Life in the Southern Seas,* London.

Inglis, John, 1890. *Bible Illustrations from the New Hebrides,* London.

Koskinen, Aarne A., 1953. *Missionary Influence as a Political Factor in the Pacific Islands,* Helsinki.

Lambert, Pierre, 1900. *Moeurs et superstitions des Néo-Calédoniens,* Noumea.

Leenhardt, Maurice, 1922. *La Grande Terre, Mission de Nouvelle Calédonie,* Paris.

—, 1923. 'La Mission des Loyalty et de Nouvelle Calédonie', *Un Siècle en Afrique et en Océanie 1822-1922,* Paris.

—, 1930. *Notes d'ethnologie Néo-Calédonienne,* Paris.

Leenhardt, Raymond, 1953. 'La Premiere Mission en Nouvelle Calédonie d'après le Journal de Ta'unga', *Le Monde Non-Chrétien* (n.s.), vol. 28, pp. 430-43.

—, 1957. *Au Vent de la Grande Terre,* Paris.

London Missionary Society, London, 1827-98. Letters, Journals and Reports from South Seas Missions.

—, Rarotonga, 1839-98. Record of graduates from Takamoa Theological College, Rarotonga.

Lovett, Richard, 1899. *History of the London Missionary Society 1795-1895,* 2 vols., London.

McFarlane, Samuel, 1873. *The Story of the Lifu Mission,* London.

Maretu, 1871. Manuscript account of Cook Islands history, Rarotonga (PS).

Maude, H. E., 1958. 'In Search of a Home', *Journal of the Polynesian Society,* vol. 67, pp. 104-31.

—, and Crocombe, Marjorie, 1962. 'Rarotongan Sandalwood. An ethnohistorical reconstruction', *Journal of the Polynesian Society,* vol. 71, pp. 32-56.

Morgan, H. J., 1961. Personal communication of 22.3.1961.

Murray, A. W., 1841. Journal 25 Feb.-13 Apr. 1841 (SSJ).

—, 1863. *Missions in Western Polynesia,* London.

—, 1874. *Wonders of the Western Isles,* London.

—, 1876. *Forty Years' Mission Work in Polynesia and New Guinea,* London.

—, 1885. *The Martyrs of Polynesia,* London.

Murray, A. W. and Turner, G., 1845. Journal of a Deputation to the New Hebrides and New Caledonia . . . 1845 (SSJ).

Native Land Court, 1903-13. Minute Books, vols. 1, 4, and 7.

Neems, Hugh, 1962. Personal communication of 30.3.1962.

New Zealand Parliamentary Papers (A3), 1901. Wellington.

O'Reilly, Patrick, 1953a. *Calédoniens: Répertoire bio-bibliographique de la Nouvelle-Calédonie,* Paris.

—, 1953b. 'Le teacher Rarotongien, Ta'unga', *Journal de la Société des Océanistes,* vol. 9, pp. 364-6.

—, 1955. *Bibliographie de la Nouvelle Calédonie,* Paris.

Papeiha, c.1830. Manuscript on the introduction of Christianity to the Cook Islands, Rarotonga (PS).

Person, Yves, 1953. *La Nouvelle Calédonie et l'Europe 1774-1854,* Paris.

Pitman, Charles, 1827-54. Journal (ML).

Powell, Thomas, 1890. 'The Story of Alele', *Journal and Proceedings of the Royal Society of New South Wales,* vol. 24, pp. 203-5.

Pratt, George, 1878. *A Grammar and Dictionary of the Samoan Language,* London.

—, and Fraser, John, 1891. 'The Kings of Manu'a and Samoa', translated by the Reverend G. Pratt with introduction and notes by Dr John Fraser, *Journal and Proceedings of the Royal Society of New South Wales for 1891,* vol. 25, pp. 133-40.

Pritchard, W. T., 1866. *Polynesian Reminiscences,* London.

Prout, Ebenezer, 1843. *Memoirs of the Life of the Rev. John Williams, Missionary to Polynesia,* London.

Samoan Reporter (periodical), 1845-57.

Savage, Stephen, 1916. 'Ko tetai korero teia e aru i te korero no te Kau Ta'unga' [A Supplementary Account of the Priesthood], Rarotonga (NLC).

Shineberg, D., 1967. *They Came for Sandalwood,* Melbourne.

Slatyer, Thomas, 1842. 'Journal of a Voyage in the Camden from Samoa, among the New Hebrides . . . 1842' (ML).

Tamarua, 1892. Lineage Book of the Ngati Tamarua, Rarotonga (CTC).

Taraare, Teariki, *c.*1870. 'No More-Ta'unga i Avana' [About More Ta'unga at Avana], contained in a manuscript history of Rarotonga (PS).

Ta'unga, 1833a. 'A Specimen of Native Writing, Rarotonga, July 1833'. A paper 3 pages in length, being a translation of verses 22 to 41 of Chapter 14 of the Gospel according to St Mark. Sent to LMS Headquarters in London by Pitman with a covering note dated 15.7.1833 (SSL).

—, 1833b. Letter of 3 pages to Pitman dated 9.9.1833 (SSL).

—, 1835. Three letters written to Pitman during 1835 respecting his dismissal from service and his application to be readmitted. No copies located. Referred to in Pitman to LMS 21.7.1835 (SSL).

—, 1840. Translation of the Journeys of the Children of Israel from Tahitian into Rarotongan. Translated during 1840. No copy located. Referred to in Pitman to LMS 20.6.1843. (SSL).

—, 1841. Letters to Pitman during 1841 respecting his future ambitions and desire to accompany Matatia on his next mission voyage. No copies preserved. Referred to in Pitman, Journal 9.8.1841 (ML).

—, 1842a. 'Te Aerenga o Barakoti ma i te kave aere i nga Orometua Rarotonga e te tutaka aere i te au enua etene, te rai i tataia e Ta'unga' [The Trip of Buzacott and Others to Take Rarotongan Teachers and to Inspect the Heathen Islands, Mostly Written by Ta'unga], *Te Puna Vai Rarotonga,* vol. 1, Mar. 1843, pp. 2-9. A copy of this publication, which was produced by the Mission Press at Rarotonga, is held at the Mitchell Library, Sydney.

—, 1842b. 'Te Toenga o te tuatua no te aerenga o Barakoti ma i tataia e Ta'unga' [The Balance of the Story of Buzacott's Trip as Written by Ta'unga], *Te Puna Vai Rarotonga,* vol. 1, no. 2, June 1843, pp. 12-15.

—, 1842c. Journal of his first three months' stay in New Caledonia in 1842, translated by Buzacott (19 pages). No copy of original vernacular document located (LMS).

—, 1842d. Vocabulary of the Tuauru language. No copy preserved. Referred to in Buzacott to LMS 4.1.1843 (SSL).

—, 1842-5. Journal of three years' stay on New Caledonia 1842-5. Abandoned at Tuauru in 1845 when compulsorily taken off owing to proposed attack from Isle of Pines. No copy preserved. Referred to in Pitman to LMS 6.8.1845 (SSL).

—, 1846a. Manuscript of 16 pages addressed to Pitman at Rarotonga. Written on the island of Mare on 9.2.1846 (PS).

—, 1846b. *No te au enua etene i aere ia e te pai orometua 1846* [About the Heathen Lands Visited by the Mission Ship in 1846]. Pages 40-3, describing conditions on the island of Mare; pages 45-50 about conditions on Lifu; and pages 51-60 on his experiences in New Caledonia, were all written by Ta'unga. This book, 65 pages in length, was printed at the Mission Press, Rarotonga, in 1847. The only known copy in existence is held by the New York Public Library. Only a part of his account was published, the balance (referred to on page 51) has not been located.

—, 1847a. Manuscript of 43 pages addressed to Pitman at Rarotonga, completed on 18.1.1847, shortly after Ta'unga's return from Melanesia (PS).

—, 1847b. 'Cannibalism in New Caledonia', *The Missionary Magazine and Chronicle,* vol. 12, pp. 162-3. This was written by Pitman on the basis of information given to him by Ta'unga (LMS).

—, 1847c. *Kange vi o Jehova, vi me ti te mo naevure Duauru.* This was a book of scripture extracts written in the Tuauru dialect for mission work. It was 24 pages in length and printed by William Gill at the Mission Press, Rarotonga, in 1847. No copy located.

—, 1847d. *Elementary Work in the New Caledonian Language.* This was also printed at the Mission Press in Rarotonga in 1847. No copy located.

—, 1848. A detailed account of the visit of Matuku to Tuauru, sent to Pitman and referred to in the latter's letter to LMS 1.12.1848 (SSL). No copy preserved.

—, 1849-72. Regular letters to Powell, his superior at Pango Pango. No copies located. Referred to in, e.g., Powell to LMS 12.1.1860 (SSL).

—, 1862. Manuscript of 24 pages dated Manu'a 19.5.1862, written at the request of W. Wyatt Gill concerning affairs at the Manu'a mission station (PS).

—, 1870. Letter dated 29.8.1870 to W. Wyatt Gill replying to questions about history and religion of pre-contact Manu'a (PS).

—, c.1871. Account of Rarotongan settlement given to John Fraser and published in the *Journal of the Polynesian Society*, vol. 6, pp. 72-3.

—, c.1870-5. History of Manu'a. Not located but referred to in Terei and Savage 1916, p. 35.

—, 1879. Manuscript of 40 pages dated 28.7.1879, concerning his work and the way of life in New Caledonia in 1842-5 (PS).

—, 1880a. Manuscript of 3 pages dated 13.1.1880, describing the preservation of breadfruit in pits in Samoa (PS).

—, 1880b. Letter of 4 pages dated 21.8.1880 addressed to W. Wyatt Gill (PS). The main significance of this letter is that it is a covering letter for a manuscript he is lending to Gill about New Caledonia and Mare, and which he asks Gill to return. The manuscript referred to has not been located.

—, 1888. *Bibilia Tapu Ra*, the Holy Bible as translated into Rarotongan in the 1888 version by Ta'unga and the Reverend W. Wyatt Gill.

—, 1892. 'Volcanic Phenomena in Samoa in 1866', *Proceedings of the Australasian Association for the Advancement of Science*, vol. 4, pp. 440-1 (as translated by Thomas Powell and presented by Dr John Fraser).

—, 1896. *Te Akapapa Anga i te Tuatua Tapu*, a scripture history of 297 pages translated from Samoan to Rarotongan by Ta'unga, the Samoan version having been translated from English by George Turner. Printed and published by the London Missionary Society, Mangaia, 1896.

—, n.d. 'Ko te Are Korero teia no Rata Ariki' [An Account of an Early Rarotongan Ancestor], *Journal of the Polynesian Society*, vol. 19, pp. 142-68. It is not certain whether this account was written by Ta'unga or by his son Tamuera Terei, as the author is stated to have been More Ta'unga-o-te-tini, a title name which was used by both of them.

Te Karere (newspaper), 1898.

Te Puna Vai Rarotonga (periodical), 1843.

Te Torea (newspaper), 1895.

Terei, Tamuera, 1899. Manuscript account of the origin of the priestly lines, Rarotonga (NLC).

—, 1905. Lineage Book of Ngati More Lineage, Rarotonga (NT).

—, 1909. Lineage Book of Ngati Terei Lineage, Rarotonga (NT).

—, and Haueti, Tivini (Stephen Savage), n.d. 'E Korero no te Kau Ta'unga o Rarotonga' [A History of the Priesthood of Rarotonga], translated by Tai Tekeu, Rarotonga (NLC).

—, 1916. 'E puka tuatua enua, papaanga tupuna, papaanga ariki, mataiapo, kopu tangata' [A Book about Lands, Genealogies, Chiefly Lines and Families], Rarotonga (NLC).

Thorogood, Bernard T., 1960. *Not Quite Paradise,* London.

—, 1961. Personal communications of 29.4.1961 and 19.12. 1961.

Threlkeld, L. E., 1853. 'Reminiscences', *The Christian Herald, and Record of Missionary and Religious Intelligence,* Sydney, 19.3.1853.

Turner, George, 1861. *Nineteen Years in Polynesia,* London.

—, 1884. *Samoa a Hundred Years Ago and Long Before,* London.

Williams, John, 1837. *A Narrative of Missionary Enterprises in the South-sea Islands,* London.

—, and Bourne, Robert, 1823. Narrative on the introduction of Tahitian missionaries to the Cook Islands, Tahiti (LMS).

Williams, J. C., 1866. Report to Foreign Office dated 19.7.1866 on a journey to Manu'a, Samoa (RPG).

INDEX

Aana, 19
Adultery, 71, 72, 146; by Europeans, 78; by mission teachers, 82; compensation, 106
Aitutaki, 4, 10, 12, 25n., 45, 114, 134
Aneityum (or Keamo), 23, 24n., 51, 75n., 114
Angara, 69
Anglican mission, 117
Aniwa, 23, 24
Apela, 23n.
Apia, 18, 29
Apolo, 24
Ara metua, 17n.
Arekao (Niue), 14-15
'Ari'a, *see* Karika
Arorangi, 82, 116, 146
Atamu, 23n.
Atinua clan, 49n.
Atiu, 12, 134, 136n., 145
Aualuma, 141
Avarua, 4, 133-4

Balade, 28, 29
Beniamina, 15, 16
Bible translation, 146
Botany Bay, 51, 63, 78
Bounty, 3, 4n.
Bourété, 27
Bourne, Rev. R., 4
Breadfruit, 2, 142
Bridge, Miss, 20n.

Brigand, 78n.
Brisk, H.M.S., 123
Buffalo, H.M.S., 29
Buma, 72
Burial, 49, 53, 60, 73, 74, 97-8, 146
Burupwari (Boulouparis), 57, 98
Buying and selling, *see* Trading
'Buying' of men, 60, 61, 80, 105-6
Buzacott, Rev. Aaron, 9, 10, 12, 14-20, 22-3, 30-1, 36, 40, 43-4, 51
Bwaxat lineage, 93n.

Camden, 10-25, 29, 30, 43-4
Canala, 27
Cannibalism, 36, 53, 57-9, 63, 74, 78-9, 86-95, 105, 108
Cape Bayes, 71n.
Cheyne, Captain, 75n.
Chiefs: and marriage, 102; and religion, 96-7; and tribute, 107; and warfare, 86, 90, 93-4, 106n., 108-9; Futuna, 23; Isle of Pines, 27, 30; Loyalty Islands, 78-84; New Caledonia, 31-53, 58-75; Niue, 15; Rarotonga, 1-5, 122, 141; Samoa, 118, 129, 140-4
Childbirth, 104

157

China, 63
Churches built: Manu'a, 120-1; New Caledonia, 42-3, 75n.; Olosenga, 131; Rarotonga, 8
Ciri, 64n.
Clothing, 111; Aneityum, 23; Manu'a, 131; Niue, 14; Tana, 22; Tuauru, 34, 64, 75
Coconuts, coconut oil, 35, 119-21, 127, 129
Collections for mission (Samoa), 119-20, 127, 129
Cook, Captain James, 29
Cook Island missionaries, see Katuke, Marama, Marie, Mataio, Matatia, Ngatikiri, Okotai, Opeta, Pakiao, Pa-Maretu, Rangi, Rupe, Sadaraka, Ta'unga, Teariki, Teava, Tekori, Teura, Tiavare, Tuka, Tukuau, Tutane
Creation, 66, 71, 83, 100
Cullen, Rev., 147
Cumberland, 3
Cunningham, — (planter), 8
Currency, see I'i, Mie, Ngolo, Ui

Dame, 31n., 42, 74
Dancing, 35, 37, 84
Daniela (mission teacher), see Taniela
Daniela (son of Ta'unga), 7
Davida, see Tavita
Death: causes, 4, 45-8, 63, 68, 71, 80-1; customs, 96-101 passim, 138; of Ta'unga, 146-7; of wives, 24; see also Epidemics, Sickness
D'Entrecasteaux, Captain J. A. R. Bruny, 29
Dido, H.M.S., 117
Dikadu, 57-8
Disease, see Epidemics, Sickness

Doku, see Thoku
Drummond, Rev. George, 19
Dubea (or Dumbea), 39n., 56, 57n.
Duff, 4

Ebrill, Captain, 22n., 23n., 38n., 43, 45, 47, 48, 50-2, 72
Efate, 79n., 114, 134
Elizabeth, 94
Epidemics: Isle of Pines, 37, 43, 46-9, 53; Lifu, 81; Mare, 80; Tuauru and Isle of Pines, 59-62, 73-4
Eromanga, 20-1, 134
Europeans (other than missionaries), 110, 122; Aneityum, 23; Isle of Pines, 25, 27-30, 45, 63; Lifu, 82; Mare, 78-9; Rarotonga, 3-4, 8; Rotuma, 20; Samoa, 122, 136; Tana, 22; see also Ebrill, Star

Falealili, 17n., 18
Falealupo, 19
Faleese, 23
Famine, 100
Fayawe, 84
Feasting: Isle of Pines, 44, 46; Lifu, 84; Mare, 79; New Caledonia, 31, 34-6, 66; Niue, 14; Rarotonga, 144; Samoa, 120, 126; Tana, 24
Federal Parliament of the Cook Islands, 148
Fertility motifs, 42n.
Fighting, see Warfare
Fish taboos, 108
Foods: Aitutaki, 12; Aniwa, 24; Isle of Pines, 50-1; Manu'a, 16; Mare, 84-5; New Caledonia, 35, 39; Rarotonga, 144; Rotuma, 20; Samoa, 19; Taboos, 108; Tana, 22; see also Planting of crops
Fornication, 132

Fuataiese, 24n.
Futuna, 23

Gadji, 45
Gill, Rev. William, 9, 82, 116, 122
Gill, Rev. Wyatt, 126, 135, 143, 146
Gods, 37-9, 73, 87, 96-101, 107; Makaza, 95; of New Caledonia, 39, 100-1; of Samoa, 141; of Samoa and Rarotonga, 37-8, 43, 49, 53, 63, 81; see also Idols
Goro, 64n., 69n.
Gradji, 56, 71
Gwahma, 79n.

Hawaiki, 1
Hayes, Commodore Sir John, 29
Heath, Rev. Thomas, 10n., 20-2, 25n., 29
Henry, Captain Samuel P., 29, 45n.
Henry, Rev. William, 38n., 45n.
Henry, William, jun., 45, 52
Hobart Town, 63, 64
Housing: Mare, 77; Rarotonga, 146; Samoa, 122; Tuauru, 32-3, 35, 43-4, 75n.
Huahine, 45
Huaisilin lineage, 79n.
Hutchen, Rev. J. J. K., 147
Hwenegei, see Uanakei

Iakopo, 77n.
Idols, 60, 67, 71, 73, 74, 80, 96-101 passim, 109; see also Gods
Ienikare, 48
I'i, 60, 104-5
Ina, see Sina
Iona, 23, 82
Ipeki, 24n.
Iro, 5, 103, 144
Isle of Pines (Kunie), 25-30, 37-8, 40, 43-54, 62, 70-2; attack from, 63-8, 75; customs, 86-95; proposed return to, 115-18
Ivanui, 141

Jaggar, Rev. John, 93n.
Jea, 74
Jeiue, 79, 81
Jinja, 49
Jiopa, 74
Jivamare, 69
John Williams, 75, 77, 85, 112, 113, 119
Johnston, Mr and Mrs, 20n.
Jones, Rev., 147
Josepha, 145
Journals lost, 76, 140

Kabwa, 57, 63
Kade, 48
Kadei, 48, 50
Kae, 57
Kai, 73
Kainuku, 141
Kame, 31
Kapao, 22
Kapea (or Kapia), 41, 74
Kaputeue, 3
Kara, 98
Karatyi, see Gradji
Kari, 100
Karika, 140-1
Katuke, 136
Keamo (son of Kai), 73n.
Keamo Island, see Aneityum
Ketuare, 72
Khiri, 64
Kiamo, 48
Kidnapping, 56, 86, 109
Kili, 100
Killing, 71-2; of Europeans, 78; of teachers, 80
Kokoti, 82
Komwainya, 26
Krause, Rev. E. R. W., 135
Kubigny (or Kuebine) River, 38n., 41n.

Kumima, 73
Kunie, *see* Isle of Pines

Land rights and sales, 25, 53, 146-7
Lamps (in mission churches), 18
Language: English, 146, (on Rotuma) 20; Gradji, 56; Hienghene, 93; Mare, 77, 82; Rarotonga, 146; role of native teachers, 118; Samoan, 16, 146; Tahitian, 8; Tana, 22; Tuauru, 31, 34, 41, 43, 60, 116; Uea 71; *see also* Translations
La Pérouse, Captain G. F. de G., 29
Lasalo (or Lazaro), 25n., 29, 45, 50-2
Laws (Manu'a), 119, 129
Leiataua, 20n.
Lelologa, 141
Leone, 17
Lifu, 25n., 27, 48, 77, 81, 83, 85, 112, 114
Lologa, 141
London Missionary Society: established in Tahiti and Rarotonga, 4; role in Melanesia, 117-18, 121; Samoa, 183-6; Uvea, 84
Loyalty Islands, 77-85, 86-101 *passim*, 103-11 *passim*, 113; *see also* Lifu, Mare, Uvea

Macdonald, Rev. Alexander, 18
Macfarlane, Rev. S., 25n.
Madoku, *see* Matuku
Magic, *see* Gods, Idols, Rain magic, Religious beliefs
Magnet, 22n.
Makarue, 74
Makaza, 95
Makea, 19
Makea Karika, *see* Karika
Malaetele, 141

Malietoa, 19n.
Malua (mission headquarters in Samoa), 117-18, 128-30, 135, 143
Mangaia, 134, 141, 145, 146; Mangaians, 45, 122, 126
Manono, 17n., 18, 25n., 136
'Man-stealers', 55
Manu'a, 16-18, 118-42; population, 119; revival on, 17n., 126-37
Manuao, 84
Maoate, Judge, 146
Marama, 16, 18
Mare (Nengone), 24, 49n., 76-81, 84, 114, 134
Maria, 123
Marie, 19
Marriage, 72, 102-4, 106, 108, *see also* Wives; Ta'unga's marriage, 122
Martha, 78n.
Massacre: ships at Mare, 78-9; *Star*, 43-54
Masui, 16
Mataika, 82
Mataio, 30-1, 35, 73n.
Matatia, 9, 16, 18
Matautu, 19
Matavera, 144
Matuku, 45-6, 48, 52, 67, 69, 70, 113n., 114
Maui, 45
Mauke, 145-6
Mediator role of missionaries, 123
Medicine, 80, 106-7, 122, 135
Meroz, 133
Meune, 73
Mie, 61, 104-6
Mills, Rev. William, 19
Miracles (credited to Ta'unga), 145
Mont Dore, 69n.
More genealogy, 2-3
More-ta'unga-o-te-tini, 1, 2, 4; *see also* Ta'unga
Mose, 22

Mulifanua, 25n.
Murphy, Captain, 75
Murray, Rev. A. W., 16-17, 25n., 29, 58, 75-7, 137

Naiad, 75n.
Nama, 49
Nao, 41
Naseai, 82
Nau, 41n.
Navie, 58n., 114-15
Nehemia, 16
Nengone, *see* Mare
Neutu, *see* Niuthu
New Caledonia, 26-76, 86-111; proposed return to, 116-18, 121
Newedu, 73n.
Ngao (Nyau), 49
Ngapoko, 122, 146
Ngatangiia, 5, 133
Ngati Au, 2, 146, 147
Ngatikiri, 15, 17
Ngaukhuthu, 98
Ngolo, 60, 104-5
Nisbet, Rev. Henry, 10n., 20n., 22
Niue (Arekao), 14-15, 17, 114, 126
Niuthu, 48, 51, 73
Niwa, 69
Noa, 25n., 29, 31, 34, 36, 37, 40, 48, 55, 57, 65, 72, 75, 76
Nohos, 24n.
Nono, 104
Noumea, 27-9, 36, 39, 57n., 63
Nowe, 41n.
Nu, 41n.
Nyavie, *see* Navie

Ofu, 127, 131
Okotai, 12, 136-7
Olosenga, 123, 128, 131, 136
Opeta (or Obeda), 128, 131-2, 136
Ouen Island, 100n.

Pa (Pa te ariki upoko tini), 2, 103, 146

Pa Maretu, 146
Pae (or Pwae), 36
Pago Pago, *see* Pango Pango
Paiau, 144
Pakiao, 16, 18
Pango Pango, 17, 18n., 25n.
Paoo, 15, 25, 82
Papeiha, 4
Pasan, 93, 94
Paulo, 74
Payment of missionaries, *see* Salary
Pedane, *see* Petani
Peniamina, *see* Beniamina
Petani, 74
Pitman, Rev. Charles, 5, 6, 7, 114-16, 118
Planting of crops, 97, 107-8
Poindimié, 71n.
Port St Vincent, 28, 29, 36
Pou-te-vananga-roa, 1, 2
Powell, Rev. Thomas, 121, 126, 128, 136-7
Pratt, Rev. George, 19, 126
Prayer, 37, 40, 47, 48, 63-6, 69-70, 73, 74, 98, 109-10, 114, 130
Preaching, *see* Teaching
Presbyterians, 117
Priests, 1, 59, 66, 80, 96-101 *passim*, 109; payment of, 106, 111; priestess, 95; *see also* Ta'unga
Pukapuka, 136
Putangi, 135
Pwae, *see* Pae

Raiatea, 1, 4, 18n.
Rain magic, 98-9
Rangi, 25n., 45
Rapanini, 69
Rape, 109
Rarotonga, 1-9, 83, 114-16, 132-4, 143-7
Religious beliefs: Christian, 3, 5, 6-7, 14, 20, 26, 34-42, 63-85 *passim*, 126-37 *passim*; non-Christian, 1, 3, 59-

62, 86-111 *passim*; food taboos, 108; *see also* Gods
Rengora, 45
Resurrection, 73n.
Retirement, 143-4
Revenge, *see* Vengeance
Rio, 4
Rongo, 141
Rongona, 141
Rotuma, 20, 77n.
Royle, Rev. Henry, 10n., 12, 126, 135
Rupe, 116
Rurutu, 4, 16n.

Sabbatarian practice, 34-7, 41-2, 75n.
Sadaraka, 136
Salary of missionaries, 121, 132, 144, 146
Sale of men, *see* 'Buying'
Saleimoa, 18
Saluafata, 17
Salvation, 38, 71, 83
Samoa, 9, 16-20, 26, 81, 114, 117-42; *see also* Manu'a
Samoan history, recording of, 140
Samoan missionaries, *see* Faleese, Fuataiese, Iakopo, Lasalo, Leiataua, Mose, Noa, Samuela, Sau, Simeona Taniela, Tataio, Tavita, Vaiofanga
Samoan-Rarotongan rivalry, 40, 77n., 121
Samuela (mission teacher), 23
Samuela (Ta'unga's son), *see* Tamuera Terei
Sandalwood, 25n., 30, 49, 52, 64n., 65n.
Sapapali'i, 18, 24n., 25n.
Sau, 20
Savai'i, 18, 19, 126, 136
Schools, 122; Manu'a, 119, 128-31, 138; Rarotonga, 5-6; Tuauru, 32, 35, 37, 75
Seiraunga, 82

Selwyn, Bishop of New Zealand, 117-18
Sickness, 100, 110; reasons for absence on Manu'a, 132; *see also* Epidemics
Simeona, 24
Sina, 141
Sisters, 78n.
Siuaiso, 31
Slatyer, Rev. Thomas, 10n., 17-18, 20n., 22, 24
Smoking, 119
Soko, 53
Sorcery, 73n., 109-10; *see also* Priests
Spirit house, 32
Spirit mediums, 1n.
Star, 22n., 23n., 38n., 43-54, 61
Suakatu, *see* Toakatyu
Sualo, 79n.
Sunia, Pastor Fiti, 138
Sydney, 26, 30, 43, 51

Taboos, *see* Religious beliefs
Tafagatafaga, 141
Tahaa, 4
Tahiti, 1, 4
Tairi, 144
Takamoa, 8, 9
Tamuera Terei, 123, 135, 144, 146
Tana (or Tanna), 20-4, 26, 51, 134
Tangaroa, 141
Tangiia, 1, 2
Tangiiau, 3
Taniela (from Mulifanua), 25n., 29-37, 40, 44
Taniela (from Pango Pango), 24-5
Taniela (from Tutuila), 25n.
Taniela (unidentified), 45
Taomi, 20
Tara, 70
Tataio, 24, 77n.
Tate, 32
Tattooing, 119

Tau a Nu'u, 140
Ta'u, 119, 124, 125
Ta'unga (priest), 1, 2, 5
Ta'unga (the man): genealogy and birth, 1-4; youth, 5-9; mission voyage, 10-26; first three months at Tuauru, 30-42; removal to Mare, 77-81; visit to Lifu, 81-5; return to Rarotonga, 112-16, 143-4; legends about, 138-40, 145; stay in Samoa, 16-20, 117-42; at Mauke, 145; retirement and death, 144-8
Taura atua, 1n.
Tavita (or Davida), 24
Tawainedre, 78n.
Te Puna Vai, 131
Teachers, role of, 118
Teaching, 37, 42, 44, 69, 73, 75; on Lifu, 83; on Mare, 77-9; on New Caledonia, 30-42 *passim*, 69-76; on Rarotonga, 5, 8-9; *see also* Schools
Teanini, 7
Teariki, 136
Teariki Taia, 3
Teava, 17
Tekari, 144
Tekori, 18
Terei Tamatapu Mataiapo, 122
Teuea, 70; *see also* Teuvea
Teura, 44, 48, 55, 57, 58, 72
Teuvea (or Te Wea), 40
Theft, 71; compensation, 106; Manu'a, 132; Tana, 22; Tuauru, 31
Theological college: Rarotonga, 8; Samoa, *see* Malua
Thio, 57
Thoine, *see* Toine
Thoku, 55
Threlkeld, Rev. L. E., 4, 18n.
Tiavare, 145
Tikoru, 14
Time, concepts of, 20n.

Tinomumu, 34, 70
Titikaveka, 5, 8, 132-3, 144
Tivaoku, 74
Tiwaka, 71
Toakatyu (or Suakatu), 36
Toine, 73, 74
Tongans in Loyalty Islands, 79, 82
Tonggo, *see* Tungoe
Touru, 27, 29, 45n.; *see also* Matuku
Trading, 49, 78, 111
Translations (by Ta'unga), 8, 43, 116, 146
Tuauru: abandonment of mission, 75-6; establishment of mission, 26-42, 55-8, 63-75; return to, 85, 112-13; war with Noumea, 63-6
Tufulele, 25n.
Tui Aana, 19n.
Tui Manu'a, 136, 141, 144
Tuji, 101
Tuka, 135, 144
Tukuau, 15, 18
Tulifua, 140
Tungoe (or Tonggo), 39, 100-1
Turi, 141
Turner, Rev. George, 10n., 20n., 22, 75-7, 117, 146
Tutane, 15, 18
Tutapu, 1
Tutuila, 16-17, 119, 126, 128

Uadengeji, 48, 49
Uadota (or Watota), 30-1, 41, 45-8, 53, 64, 73, 74
Uaemu (Wamu), 74
Uaima, 48
Uaise (Ueiji), 72n.
Uakutamie, 70
Uanakakame, 78-9
Uanakei, 84
Uao, 55n., 70
Uaoia, 70
Uaraui, 48

Uaroku (or Wareku), 41
Uea (Uvea?), 71
Ueiji, 48, 72
Ui, 60, 104-5
Uima, 48
Ukupore (Ukapwere), 49
Unia, 31n., 40n., 49, 70n., 72
Unihini (or Unin), 71
United Secession Synod of
    Scotland, 118
Upolu (Samoa), 17n., 18, 19,
    119, 135-6
Uvea, 71n., 82-5, 114

Vahapata, 4
Vaiapi, 128
Vaiofanga, 22n.
Vakune, 70
Vao, 45, 51
Vengeance, 49, 71, 72, 91, 97,
    106, 108-10
Vindictiveness, 86, 108-10
Visionary experience, 139-40
Volcanic eruption, 123-4

Wakun, 55
Wamu, *see* Uaemu
Wanakam, *see* Uanakakame
Wao, 70

Wareku, *see* Uaroku
Warfare, 86-93, 96-8, 101,
    105; causes, 59, 61, 68n.,
    74, 86, 108; Isle of Pines,
    27, 51-2, 75; Manu'a, 123,
    136-7; Mare, 25, 79-80, 84;
    Tuauru, 31, 35-6, 42n., 55,
    57, 61, 63-5, 91, 112-13
Watota, *see* Uadota
Weapons, 22, 46-7, 56-7, 64-6,
    82, 98, 101, 113
Weco clan, 41n.
Wedji, *see* Ueiji
Weleni, Captain, 64
Wenyi, *see* Ueiji
Widows, treatment of, 24
Williams, Rev. John, 4, 16,
    21
Witchcraft, *see* Gods, Idols,
    Sorcery
Wives, 24, 109; taken by
    Europeans, 78; taken in
    war, 93; *see also* Marriage
Woodin, Captain, 64n.

Yate, 38n., 55-8
Yeiw, *see* Jeiue

Zekaria, 25, 82

*Text set in 10pt on 11pt Baskerville on Burnie MF Printing
Printed by Riall Print Pty Ltd, Melbourne,
for the Australian National University Press*

Printed and manufactured in Australia